The Muslim Conquest of Spain

and the Legacy of Al-Andalus

Shahnaz Husain

Taha Publishers Ltd.
www.taha.co.uk

Published by:
Ta-Ha Publishers Ltd.
1 Wynne Road
London SW9 0BB

Website: http://www.taha.co.uk
Email: sales@taha.co.uk

By: Shahnaz Husain
Edited, with Glossary, by: Isla Rosser-Owen
General Editor: Dr Abia Afsar-Siddiqui
Typeset: Yasin Mohammad Shaikh

A catalogue record of this book is available from the British Library.

ISBN 1 842000 39 X

Printed in England by: De-Luxe Printers, London NW10 7NR

Email: deluxeprinters1@aol.com

"It is He who is revealed in every face,
sought in every sign,
gazed upon by every eye,
worshipped in every object of worship,
and pursued in the unseen and the visible.
Not a single one of His creatures can fail to find Him
in its primordial and original nature."

(Muhyuddin ibn 'Arabi, *Futuhatu-l Makkiyyah*)

Dedication

For my husband, Rakib

For Linda, Ifti and Farid

Good friends and members of a
productive, supportive family

CONTENTS

PART II: THE LEGACY OF AL-ANDALUS

Author's Note

Many thanks are due to Junaid Doja and Leesa Khalid for their words of wisdom and for their encouragement in writing this book. Thanks also to Rakib for supporting me with his time and for encouraging me to pursue my love of writing. A big '*Jazakallah*' goes to my sister, Linda, for proofreading the material and for being my best critic. Finally, thanks go to my three children, who inspired me to start writing in the first place because I felt there was not enough material available in Muslim bookshops dealing with Islamic history.

PREFACE

Today we live in troubled times. As the twentieth century has drawn to a close and we have entered a new millennium, we should pause to reflect for a moment on what the future holds in terms of Islam. Islam has come a long way from its fledgling years, when a small band of dedicated men and women in the Arabian Desert strove and died for a belief system that still holds firm today.

Incredibly, this religion that had such humble beginnings is now the world's fastest growing religion – *al-hamdu lillah* – and the Prophet's ﷺ Message is being embraced by millions of people all over the world – a sure sign that he did not fail. After all, how could he? He was Allah's chosen Prophet ﷺ. So we must now ask ourselves, are we living up to the expectations of our beloved Muhammad ﷺ? Sadly, I fear that the answer is no.

Times have changed markedly from when Islam was first instituted. The world is a very complex place today. Yet we are reminded in the Quran that the tenets of the faith, published over a thousand years ago, are as fitting now as when first chartered. But, the world is not the same place, and the heroes and personalities who were once shining beacons of light, and who were adulated throughout the Muslim and non-Muslim worlds, have sadly been forgotten or replaced by new non-Muslim heroes for our children to follow.

Today we live in a world of images that bombard us twenty-four hours a day. They exist in our homes, at work, on billboards as we go shopping and, most disastrously, on TV. The images themselves are often of modern day heroes from the worlds of cinema, sport, fashion and music, and unfortunately, many of these are considered to be our icons and gurus for the twenty-first century. What can we possibly teach our children if these people are celebrated as the role models of today? What do they depict? That money and fame are the criteria to life and success, and that the *dunya*, the life of this world, is the be all and end all of existence? This is the complete antithesis of Islam. Islam teaches that the *dunya* is just an ephemeral place for the traveller, whose real home is in the *akhirah* or here-after. We are told quite categorically not to strive for the *dunya* unnecessarily. We are here simply to fulfil certain functions that the Almighty has commanded us to do and then, when we go to our graves and 'open our eyes', our real lives will begin.

Muslim Role Models

So how do we shape our children's thinking with regards to role models? Where to next? School is a possibility – after all, this is where we read of the great men of vision. Yet, a closer look at such figures of Western history as Stalin or Christopher Columbus brings disappointment. Most of the men of Stalin's kind were not driven by Socialist idealism, but by their own obsession with power. Whatever courage and talent they showed were simultaneously characterised by inordinate levels of cruelty. However, what is most worrying is that for a long time the West depicted such men in glorious terms as if they were promoting the philosophies and idealism that it held dear. Similar parallels can be identified today. Consequently, present day school curricula marginalise the impact of other peoples and cultures in the formation of world civilisation, which in today's multi-cultural society seems a little odd.

Sadly, we are also beginning to see that in some Muslim countries the vital role of the Islamic conquests and the great policies, literature and sciences of our past now plays second fiddle to Western thoughts on the same subjects. For example, Augustus Caesar is admired for his policies and administrative skills, which had propagated internal peace and prosperity for two centuries. However, no mention is made of the pivotal figure of the Khalifa (Caliph) 'Ali, whose wise policies and administrative brilliance were the bases of the success and permanence of his Islamic government following the death of Prophet Muhammad ﷺ, and indeed they continue to form the framework for policymaking today. The establishment of the Welfare State and the granting of pensions in the United Kingdom are both policies that have been modified directly from those of the Muslims and they now endure as a part of all Western forms of government.

We read about the brilliant military prowess of Napoleon or Genghis Khan and their vast conquests. What is less known is that the greatest of military soldiers and strategists in history was Khalid ibn al-Walid. His brilliance led him to be named the 'Unsheathed Sword of Allah', a title bestowed on him by Allah (SWT) Himself. What other man in history can boast that the Creator gave him his military title! During the Caliphates of Abu Bakr, 'Umar and 'Uthman, Khalid ibn al-Walid led the Muslim Army and he never lost a battle throughout his numerous campaigns across neighbouring lands, which included Syria and Egypt.

When he was dying, he was most perturbed that he had to die in his bed "like an old woman", as he put it, and that he was not to go out in a show of glory on the battlefield. When the Companion Bilal went to see him he expressed such disappointment, but, sanguinely, Bilal told him that as he was 'the Sword of Allah' no human being would ever be able to take him down. As a general, his astute tactical manoeuvres and strategic planning were unsurpassed, and many of his methods still form the bases of modern military strategy.

The Importance of Muslim History

Therefore, in perspective, it is important for us as parents to educate our children about the vast, untapped history out there that is just waiting for us to brush off the cobwebs that cover it and to rediscover the stories that have so far been lost in the annals of time.

One further factor that still seems to be a problem, and one which I highlighted four years ago when writing *Muslim Heroes of the Crusades*[1] , is that the focus for Islamic history in most bookshops still predominately centres around the time of the Prophet ﷺ. But, Islamic history goes way beyond that period. Some outstanding personalities, all of whom did incredible things for their faith, can be found throughout the twelfth, thirteenth and fourteenth centuries. Still no one is writing about these people and our children's lives are being taken over by all the wrong role models. No one can blame the *kuffar* as they have their own agenda and they are sticking to them, meanwhile sweeping up the world in their brand of magic. The Muslims, in the meantime, are sitting back and they are not taking the initiative whilst our children go astray.

---

[1] Husain, Shahnaz, *Muslim Heroes of the Crusades*, Ta-Ha Publishers Ltd., London, 1998.

Today, when life in virtually every part of the world is confused by the pull of conflicting non-Islamic values and societal influences, Muslim youngsters are growing up under immense pressure coming from all directions. It should be the goal of every Muslim parent to nurture in their child a sound personality and to equip their children to handle the demands of modern life in an Islamic fashion. However, such essentials do not just come from obedience to rituals, or through simply following directives based on *halal* and *haram*. Ritualistic practice alone is not the answer. A wide spectrum of knowledge encompassing other areas is also needed.

Let us take charge of our legacy

Hence, it is vital to look back at our history to forge a common identity and to take back the legacy that is rightfully ours; to infuse our children with pride and a love of Islam, which can only spring from an understanding of the people who were once living examples of an unfailing submission to Allah. By writing about the brave men and women of the past we nurture the ground for future generations. It will furnish us with models of behaviour to provide direction for young children, who will become men and women of action and good will, *insha Allah*.

We must reverse, and diminish, the damage done to our Prophet's ﷺ legacy by the non-Muslims. For too long now our youth have felt either apathy towards Islam, or a complete disregard for it. In their ignorance they only perceive what the media makes them believe – that, for example, it is the Muslims who instigate oppressive regimes that discourage modernisation. That is why it is heartening to know that, as long as remarkable personalities exist, the spirit of Islam is alive to pass on to our children. For, it is due to these great men and women that we are able to follow examples now that our beloved Prophet ﷺ is no longer personally with us to guide us on a daily basis through this transient life to the Hereafter.

Shahnaz Husain
Essex, England, 2004

INTRODUCTION

The Muslim Conquest of the Iberian Peninsula[2] is a landmark event in history. It began in the year 710 CE, and eventually led to almost total control, by the Muslims, of the entire region. Muslim governance of this region then opened up a wealth of learning to an area that had fallen into decline after the Romans had been ousted from power by the Visigoths, and it surpassed anything that Western Europe had yet seen.

The Muslim rule, by the 'Moors' of North Africa and others from the Middle East, lasted for almost one thousand years. In that time, a golden example was set of enlightened and just leadership, and the era also brought remarkable prosperity and some marvellous feats of engineering, art, science and literature to a region that had once been a poor backwater of the furthermost part of the Roman Empire.

To understand why the Muslims came to this region it is important for us to look at the overall history and geography of the area.

Modern Spain occupies most of the Iberian Peninsula, some 85 per cent of it. The term 'Iberian' has been used since pre-Roman times to describe the multi-racial culture that has always existed in this region.

Geographically, the north-eastern part of Spain is bordered by the Pyrenees Mountains, which stretch for about 240 miles,

---

[2] The term used to refer to what are now Spain and Portugal. The use of 'Spain' at this stage is an anachronism as Spain the country did not come into existence for several hundred years, and only after the Muslims had left the region.

cutting the country off from the rest of Europe. Thus, a rugged natural barrier is formed between Spain and France. The north coast faces the Atlantic Ocean and the Bay of Biscay, while to the south-east lies the Mediterranean. To the south is the short crossing from Spain to Africa, known as The Straits of Gibraltar, and it was by way of this route that the Muslims had first made their historic crossing into the province that came to be called 'Al-Andalus'.

Spain is often mistakenly thought of as an entirely hot and dusty country. In fact it has a wide range of climatic conditions. In the centre of the country the summers are extremely hot and the winters fairly cold; while in the south the temperatures are similar to those of North Africa and can rise to 115 degrees centigrade, something that no doubt made the region attractive to the many Muslims who flocked there. The different climatic conditions enabled the growing of a variety of foodstuffs from oranges and pomegranates, to peaches, lemons and grapes, all introduced to the region by the Muslims and which are now still grown all over the country. In the north, the mild and temperate climate is ideal for growing potatoes, together with many other root vegetables and they predominate along the mild, moist northern coastal plains.

Spain is a country whose people are descended from many ethnic groups because of the country's complicated history and culture. For more than 2,500 years the region has struggled against wave after wave of successive invaders, starting with the Phoenicians and then moving on to the Romans and the Visigoths and, finally in the eighth century, ending with the Muslims who swarmed over from North Africa and founded a major civilisation that lasted for centuries. This conquest effectively made the Iberian Peninsula into a Muslim country. Many Spaniards today carry Moorish blood in them. The Muslim legacy can be found everywhere, from the names of local rivers and towns such as Tarifa, to the use of exotic spices and colours in the food. Local pottery too has a distinctive Eastern flavour to it. Remnants of the Muslim influence are more pronounced in the countryside where some of the older women will still wear scarves and do the family cooking outside.

When the Muslims invaded the region over a thousand years ago, much of Europe was in ignorance about basic facts of life, such as hygiene, medicine, reading and writing, and many of the other things that we take for granted today. For example, the use of water, even for simple things such as personal cleanliness, was viewed by some with suspicion and considered to be a heathen custom.

The Muslims, at the opposite end of the spectrum, demonstrated the wondrous effects that the uses of water could achieve in, for example, irrigation in some of the drier, more inhospitable areas of Al-Andalus. They created 'gardens of Eden', and this creative genius can still be seen today in the magnificent palace of the old Muslim rulers of Granada - the edifice known as the Alhambra, where the gardens are still perfumed by the delicate scent of flowers, and are accompanied by the twinkling sound of the fountains.

The Muslim Conquest that took place over a thousand years ago had an enormous impact and it has left a lasting legacy in Spain, the light of which still shines to this day.

***

Part I

The Muslim Conquest of Spain

CHAPTER ONE

- 'Paradise on Earth' -

Al-Andalus has at various times been called by different writers, 'Paradise on Earth', 'Heaven's Gate' and a variety of other enchanting names to compliment its beauty.

The modern province of Andalusia, which covers most of Southern Spain and is where much of the Muslim conquests and settlements initially took place, begins after the Sierra Morena, a range of mineral-enriched mountains darkly covered in forests that cut off the region from the rest of the country.

The region stills betrays the legacy of its Muslim past. Indeed, once people have crossed these mountains past La Mancha, which is a barren, scorched, desert-like area, into Andalusia, the scenery changes as dramatically as if they had crossed from Europe into Africa. The arid environment left behind in La Mancha is replaced by running streams, reflected sunlight dancing on glistening water, wild flowers growing in abundance, and a general feeling that you have arrived somewhere warm and sensual. In fact, the beauty of Andalusia captivates the eyes and appears all the more enchanting in contrast to the scenery just left behind.

Travellers almost feel that they have left Spain altogether and that they have entered a different continent, so vastly different are the vegetation, culture and climatic conditions that prevail. Nearly eight hundred years of Islamic rule no doubt adds to the ambience as the area is scattered with palm trees, cacti, Eastern architecture and exotic foodstuffs.

The beauty of the scenery can be summed up in the words of a member of the Polish Royal Family, who had visited the region in 1611: "When we entered Andalusia tired after the monotonous desert we had just crossed, our senses were amply restored by the beauty, joy and abundance of products of this country... I thought I was in Paradise."

The Almighty in His Wisdom and Generosity not only blessed the lands of Southern Spain with many resources, the shorelines too are plentifully supplied with varieties of fish, such as swordfish, sardines and cod, as well as some more exotic breeds like chanquete, octopus and squid.

All of these factors naturally appealed to the senses of any people who arrived there, the Muslims being no exception.

However, the Muslims did not just decide to barbarically invade another country, as is often the story depicted – unfairly – in inaccurate accounts of Islamic history. In fact, they were invited to come with repeated requests that they help reconcile the various local parties at loggerheads with each other. They had had no interest in invading the Iberian Peninsula prior to being summoned to settle a disagreement between two Christian factions, who had been competing for the sovereignty of the state. Although the aim of calling upon the Muslims was to hire them as mercenaries, in fact they ended up staying as the region's new rulers for nearly a thousand years.

***

CHAPTER TWO

- Roman Rule of the Iberian Peninsula -

Prior to the arrival of the Muslims, successive rulers had committed unspeakable crimes against their people. The Romans were the first major conquerors to arrive, although they were eventually weakened by minor encroachments made by ethnic groups such as the Alans and Suevi. The Visigoths were the last group of peoples to invade before the Muslims. The indigenous people had fared poorly under both the Romans and the Visigoths and had become resigned to their fate. A few heroic attempts were made to shake off the shackles under which they suffered, but most of these failed while the repressive measures that were meted out after abortive attempts at freedom were more savage even than the conditions they had endured before.

When the Romans first arrived in the Peninsula they were hardy soldiers used to a rough life and committed to the idea of expanding and maintaining their empire in good order. They were determined to make 'Hispania' into another profitable and prominent province of the Roman Empire. Administrative bodies were set up to oversee the running of the Province, which had been divided into various districts.[3] Each district had to provide a certain amount of revenue for the upkeep of the state and, consequently, the money that poured in from the collection of taxes helped to run the country. However, the Roman Empire, which had been an incredible

---

[3] The Romans had a number of provinces that fell under the overall name of 'Hispania'.

force for four centuries, began to go into decline from c. 350 CE onwards and, as with so many waning empires throughout history, corruption and moral laxity soon prevailed.

The Romans had set up a social hierarchy. At the very top were the *latifundia* – an elite group of landowners with vast estates. After these came the chief magistrates and the wealthy businessmen. None of these groups paid taxes. Below these were the middle classes – the *curiales* – on which the burden of maintaining the state fell as the main tax-paying group. Finally, at the bottom of the social structure lay the slaves in all their misery.

The *latifundia* lived a life of immense luxury. They erected palatial homes for themselves with splendid gardens where they spent their days entertaining guests or being amused by large numbers of dancing girls. They would not have been able to sustain a life like this had it not been for the *curiales*, who were compelled to maintain them in their luxury.

However, some significant changes were underway as Christianity had begun to grow and to take root within the Roman Civilisation. Constantine had made a ruling that in one fell swoop took away what little power the *curiales* had left. He had effectively seized their property by decreeing that any *curial* who owned more than 25 acres of land, but was not a member of one of the privileged classes, must make up any shortfall in the local taxes from his own pocket in order to maintain state expenses. On another occasion, he also created a statute that deemed him to be the actual owner of their land. The *curiales* became mere overseers. Burdened with such crippling liabilities, many *curiales* abandoned their estates and joined other professions in order to sustain their families.

Their once respected and dignified occupation had been reduced to one of mortifying degradation under tyranny. Life had become so hard that many men fled to the countryside as professional bandits, roaming the forests in bands ready to prey on unsuspecting wealthy travellers.[4]

Such was the condition of the Iberian Peninsula under the Romans. However, with time, the power of the Roman Empire continued to decline further. This was most obvious in the outermost regions of the Empire, where law and order was breaking down and the threat posed by foreign barbarians was becoming an ever-increasing problem.

In 457 CE, the threat of an invasion had become imminent from a Germanic people known as the Visigoths – a semi-autonomous federation (*foederatus*) of the Roman Empire – but the state of affairs in the region was so poor that most of the population appeared to care very little. The slaves believed that their lot in life could not possibly become worse and the middle classes were dissatisfied with the burdens and bankruptcy imposed upon them, as well as the fact that they had been maintaining the state but reaping little of the benefits. Finally, the wealthy nobles, perhaps worn out by debauchery, slovenly habits and years of inactivity, were not in any condition to lift their rusty swords let alone lead a concerted effort to banish the invaders.

Therefore, it was hardly surprising that when the Visigoths had finally arrived they were met with little resistance. City after city capitulated with little or no hindrance. In fact, it is

---

[4] It was these bandits that had become so numerous at a previous stage that Julius Caesar had had to lead an army against them to quell their numbers.

a testimony to the state and condition of Roman Iberia that no city attempted an extensive campaign. Gates flew open and the barbarian hordes stumbled in. The Hispano-Roman rulers, sunk in debauchery, drunkenness and a cocooned existence, knew only too well what resistance meant. Carnage and bloodshed, towns burnt and citizens carried away as slaves were all possibilities, while those left behind would face starvation and hunger. Decadent as they had become, the stirrings of any brave resistance were sadly lacking. They felt it was better to succumb and so, humbly, they submitted to their conquerors.

***

CHAPTER THREE

- The Invasion of the Visigoths -

The Visigoths, also known as the Western Goths, were a Germanic people that had overrun most of the Iberian region in the sixth century. Having arrived in the north, they immediately began a campaign of massacring and looting on their destructive path through the region. One of the first towns to be ravaged was Braga, where many of the citizens were carried off into slavery. The next major town to be attacked was Astorga. Here, the barbarian hordes were more ruthless. They lay waste to the entire town, carrying off women and children and setting fire to churches and homes.

Meanwhile, news had spread fast that the invaders had arrived and were in no mood for compromise or arbitration. As panic began to spread, sporadic attempts were finally made to defend the region in some of the small castles and hamlets, such as the one near Ponferrada where the people had managed to keep out the Visigoths by staging a siege. Other parts of the country were not so lucky. Slowly and methodically the Visigoths captured the whole of Iberia, destroying major cities, burning, pillaging and looting.

Amidst all of this, there was one section of society untroubled by the impending destruction of their country. They were the clergy. They looked upon the invasion with some optimism, feeling that the ruination of the old Roman Province could be no bad thing. Pagan principles still had some roots in Iberian culture and this, of course, was detrimental to the long-term objectives of the Catholic Church. Much of the region had only recently become familiar with Christianity following conversion. Moreover, sections of Iberian society had also become Arian Christians, whose Unitarian beliefs – which rejected the Doctrine of the Trinity – were contrary to Catholicism.

The main body of Hispano-Roman society was still ignorant, therefore, of Catholic principles, such as the Trinity, and so the destruction of this 'Old World Order' meant little to the priests. This has been proved by letters and documents from various ecclesiastical bodies that have survived from this period and which speak positively of the invasion.

For the Catholic Church, the primary concern would always be whether the invasion was beneficial to its long-term objectives or not. It mattered little to many clergymen that people were being murdered, that homes were being destroyed and families ripped apart. So long as the Church could maintain its grip on the areas that mattered, which included state legislation and court politics, the invasion was not seen as the disaster it had been elsewhere. Of course, not all elements of the Church agreed, but history tends to document the majority opinion and the majority of the clerics seemed unconcerned. [5]

As one region after another fell to the barbarians, some of the terrified inhabitants of the region had attributed the destruction of their society to the neglect of their previous Roman gods. Had they performed the sacrificial rites and carried out their pagan duties properly this might never have

[5] This has been documented by the historian Hodgkin in his book, *'Italy and her Invaders'*. Italy's history in many ways parallels that of Spain. ·

28

happened. The clergy naturally took advantage of this situation and reasoned that, for Catholicism to take root, an invasion was absolutely necessary.

Even though the clergy held these views they were, nevertheless, still unsure how the Visigoths would react to them. However, they were not to be disappointed. The Visigoths were Arian Christians and so were familiar with the tenets of Christianity before their invasion. When the priesthood reminded them that it was an act of God that had made them so successful, they meekly acceded to this argument. So doggedly did the priesthood pursue its mission to become a power in its own right that by 587 CE the Visigoth ruler, King Reccared, had been forced to renounce his former beliefs and become Catholic.

Thereafter, the hold that the bishops and high-ranking clergymen exercised over the King was complete. They made it understood that, without their intercession on behalf of the King, no favour could be found with God. King Reccared dutifully affirmed his complete allegiance to the Church and begged them to find favour with the Almighty to give precedence to his state and his affairs. Thus, the Church, at least, had finally achieved its aim: an all-powerful position in the land to command at will and be obeyed. They eventually used the converted Visigoth aristocracy to enforce the new faith onto the wider society.

The Condition of the Lower Classes

Naturally, with this shift in power, the downtrodden classes believed that their lot would finally improve. After all, the Church had for a long time condemned the evils of slavery as being abhorrent to the true spirit of Christianity. Now that the clergy (as the guardians of morality) had a measure of influence, it was believed that their previous dedication to humanity and their solicitude for the weak would mean an end to this vile institution. However, the Church in fact had made a complete turn around in its policy. An attack of amnesia assailed the ecclesiastical world as it recanted its former position.

A change of policy was effected overnight. Having gained such immense power, the Catholic Church realised that it needed the vast numbers of serfs and slaves to look after the large estates that had been gifted to it by the Crown. To allow these men freedom would mean that paid or hired labour would become necessary and this was something to be avoided. The freedom that many had dreamed of and yearned for never materialised and the institution of slavery continued to be a black cloud hanging over the Iberian horizon for many years to come.

In fact, many leading men of the cloth even went so far as to preach the benefits of human bondage. For instance, Bishop Isidore of Seville – a prominent member of the Council of Toledo – quoted Greek philosophers of old, who had stated that, "Nature has commanded some to lead and others to obey".

If anything, the condition of these people was considerably worse under the rule of the Visigoths than it had been under the Romans. They were not allowed to marry without the permission of their masters.[6] If two slaves married from neighbouring estates then their children were split between

---

[6] A similar policy was used by the Romans with regard to slave marriages.

the two estates. In this respect, the society of the Catholic Visigoths was more oppressive than that of the Romans – even Constantine had forbidden the breaking up of families as being unnecessarily cruel. Many documented records of fugitive slaves from this period have been found and they bear testament to the harsh reality of what was endured.

While the bondsmen and women suffered, the middle classes too fared little better than before. As previously, they continued to maintain the tax system out of their own pockets and with the little left over they fed their families. No farmer could sell his land without first seeking permission and meanwhile the concentration of power remained in the hands of an elite few. The rumblings of this discontent with the Catholic Church could soon be heard. As these grew audibly louder, the clergy, conscious of its failure to alleviate the people's suffering, realised that it was only a matter of time before it would be held accountable for its neglect in upholding its duties. It found a simple, expedient and time-honoured excuse to relinquish itself of blame: it was all the fault of the Jews.

***

CHAPTER FOUR

- The Iberian Jews -

According to tradition, the Jews first arrived in the Peninsula at the time of the famous Babylonian King Nebuchadnezzar, who had first taken them as his slaves from Palestine to Assyria. Others had moved to the Iberian Peninsula from the Middle East and other parts of Europe. They had been principally involved in business as merchants and artisans and had lived in relative peace in the area until the tide turned in 616 CE. Under pressure created by the Catholic Church, it was declared that all Jews were to be forcibly converted to Christianity. Those who continued to pursue the doctrines of Judaism were to be whipped and have their property confiscated. This hard-line policy led to approximately 100,000 conversions.

However, forcing people to convert to another religion does not necessarily mean they will adhere to the faith that has been thrust upon them. The Fourth Council of Toledo – a fore-runner to the infamous Spanish Inquisition – was convened to supervise the conversions and they realised just this. Jews might have been forced to convert to Christianity, but at home many continued their Mosaic practices. In the end, the Council contented itself with the fact that, in theory, mass conversions had taken place, even though in reality this was not the case.

It was also decided at the Sixth Council of Toledo that no king could be crowned unless he had sworn to uphold these laws, the enforcement of which had gone so far as to take Jewish children away from their parents to raise them as Catholics.

Columns in the Cordoba Mosque

For nearly one hundred years the Jews continued to suffer until it had become unbearable. Circa 694 CE, they organised a rebellion in collaboration with their co-religionists across the waters in the Maghrib, who had planned to band together and join their oppressed brothers in the Iberian Peninsula where a series of rebellions would break out simultaneously. However, before the plan could be executed, it was discovered. Egica, the king at the time, summoned his Council to corroborate the rumours. They, in turn, had captured a number of Jews and, after torturing confessions out of them, were able to confirm that the rebellion was indeed about to take place.

A cry of outrage ran through the court and it was decided that the measures already meted out had not been severe enough. Henceforth, it was decided that all children were to be taken away from their parents at the age of seven and baptised as Christians. Jews were not allowed to marry other Jews but only Christians. In fact, everything was done to break the morale and dignity of the Jewish people. We have little reason to doubt that these actions were taken as they have been well documented by both Jewish and Spanish historians. As one chronicler states:

"When the Muslims conquered the north-west of Africa, the Jews of Spain were groaning beneath an intolerable yoke; they ceased not to pray for their deliverance; the conquerors who set them free and granted them religious liberty, subject to the payment of a light tribute, were in their eyes saviours from heaven."

These repressive, tyrannical and cruel measures by the Catholic Visigoths meant that the majority of society was on its knees ready to support any liberator who might come along to alleviate their suffering. The time was ripe for the Muslim invasion.

***

*Detail of the Lion's Patio - **Granada** Alhambra*

*Fountains and Garden - **Granada** Generalife*

CHAPTER FIVE

- Roderick's Crime -

Count Julian lived in eighth century North Africa. He was a Christian and the Governor of Ceuta, a small Christian town still under the protection of the Byzantine Empire. As the Empire was so large it was often difficult for the more far-flung provinces to maintain close links with the capital.

Ceuta – situated on the coast of North Africa – because of its distance from Constantinople and the fact that most of North Africa by that time was Muslim, looked over the waters to the Iberian Peninsula as its closest Christian ally and friend.

It was the custom at that time for young men and women of noble birth to be sent to the Royal Court to learn about protocol and courtly etiquette. As the closest Christian kingdom was at Toledo, Julian decided to send his young daughter, Florinda, there to be educated by King Roderick's ladies in waiting.

Roderick had become the Visigoth king through a combination of treachery and murder. He had deposed the previous monarch, King Witiza. Witiza, the son of the previous King Egica, had come to the throne in 702 CE. As was the custom throughout most of Europe at that time the monarchy was mainly hereditary, though in certain cases a person could be elected into power. Witiza had succeeded to the throne after his father. When his rule was coming to an end he likewise attempted to pass it on to his son. However, certain nobles at court decided to contest his claim for political reasons and his son, Akhila, was killed in a battle between the two factions. Roderick seized power and was duly elected the new king by the nobles who had supported him. This course of action, though legal in Visigothic law, had antagonised a large influential faction at court – most notably Witiza's family who felt themselves to be the legitimate heirs to the throne.

Having become king, Roderick began his tenure well as a reasonably skilled administrator. However, with the passing of time, temptation exacerbated by wealth and power finally overcame him.

Florinda, the young daughter of Count Julian, was very beautiful. Having been at Court for a while she caught the immoral eye of King Roderick who ravaged her, forgetting the promise of protection that he had made to her father. Distressed by what had happened to her, Florinda summoned one of her servants and gave him a letter to be taken to her father. In it she detailed what had happened and begged him to come and take her away from King Roderick's roving eye.

Upon reading her message Count Julian, naturally, was beside himself with rage. He already had little regard or affection for Roderick, as his wife was the daughter of the deposed King Witiza. But with the dishonour of Florinda, his family had been doubly insulted and the bitterness that he had felt towards Roderick for so long flared up into a desire for revenge at all costs.

However, Julian knew that he could not destroy Roderick by himself and so he devised a plan with some of the other disgruntled noblemen, as well as with members of Witiza's

*Courtyard of the "Acequia" - **Granada** Generalife*

family. He had decided that the Muslims should be invited into the country. "After all, it is in the Muslim hands that the resources of manpower and weaponry needed to destroy Roderick exist," he argued with his co-conspirators. "They have the resources, we do not. If we ask them to aid us, and reward them amply, they will support our cause."

For a long time this perfidious statesman had defended Ceuta against the Muslims, but now, in his fury, he would ask them to help him depose Roderick with the Iberian lands as the reward for their co-operation. And so, as has happened so many times throughout Islamic history, the Muslims, instead of setting out to invade another country, were actually to be invited in to aid one fractious party against another.

In actual fact, although he offered these grandiose schemes so freely to the Muslim generals, it is doubtful that Julian intended to hand the country over to the Muslims entirely. It was simply an inducement. Perhaps these nobles thought that, having helped them, the Muslim armies would eventually go back to their own countries, having amassed enough booty as their reward. They thought, quite plausibly, that they would only be interested in the financial rewards on offer. However, before he could induce the Muslim generals to come to his aid, Julian had one more important plan up his sleeve. He would try to convince King Roderick that his country was soon to be attacked by bands of Moors who were about to storm across the seas.

***

CHAPTER SIX

- Julian Prepares the Ground -

Count Julian prepared himself methodically and cautiously for the plan in hand. Having received the go-ahead from his compatriots, he sailed across the water and arrived at Roderick's Court, pretending to pay homage to his lord and benefactor. Concealing his hatred and vengeful rancour, gracefully he demonstrated his allegiance to the King. Roderick, overwhelmed by the courteous honour Julian had bestowed on him, felt a little guilty about what he had done to the Governor's daughter. Showering praises on his Governor, he bade him take a seat by his side while he listened to his concerns.

Julian told the King that he had heard a rumour circulating that Muslims from North Africa would soon attack his kingdom. He added that he had come in all haste to advise him that the wisest course of action would be to send his best cavalrymen and foot soldiers to the south where they would be under Julian's command. The real intention was, of course, to remove the most capable men from Roderick's control. Meanwhile, the King would be under the impression that Julian was leading any offensive necessary to banish the invaders.

Having agreed to the plan, the King's parting request to Julian was that he send over some hawks from North Africa for him to use out hunting. Julian's cloaked reply was that he would indeed send such hawks, the type of which the King had never seen before. Leaving this cryptic clue as to what was about to happen to the kingdom, he then departed with his daughter.

CHAPTER SEVEN

- Julian Meets Musa ibn Nusayr -

On Julian's return to Ceuta, the first thing he did was to throw open the gates of the town to the Moors. Previously Julian had done nothing but exchange hostilities with them. However, that was now all in the past as he decided he would henceforth extend his hand in friendship to the Muslim Governor.

Musa ibn Nusayr, the Governor of Ifriqiya and the Muslim Maghrib, was summoned to Julian's residence. After pleasantries had been exchanged, Julian informed Musa about his change in policy and that a new era of friendship and co-operation should exist between them. Musa raised an eyebrow at the suggestion. He was, naturally, a little suspicious. "What has prompted you to take the Muslim as your friend now?" he enquired of Julian.

Julian told him about the insult to his daughter and his desire to avenge her honour. Musa, shaking his head, thought this was a poor inducement to consider risking his troops. However, Julian was a clever man. He knew that simply asking Musa to avenge his daughter's honour would not be enough, and so he filled the General's ears with tales of the beauty of the Iberian region: the fertility of the land; the rivers and mountains; the warm pleasant climate; the sumptuous palaces with their rich treasures; the towns and cities, all available for the taking. The decaying and crumbling civilisation of the Visigoths was on its knees. Musa simply had to go over and capture it and Julian would help him.

Musa finally considered that the idea might have some merit. After all, he had been invited in, Julian was willing to supply his troops with ships for the crossing, and it would be a chance to expand the boundaries of Islamic dominions. However, he was also a cautious man. "This tempting offer could in fact be a treacherous plan to ambush our men", he reasoned to his lieutenant. After some discussions, it was decided to seek further instructions from the Khalifa in Damascus.

The Role of the Khalifa

At the head of the *Ummah* at that time sat the Khalifa al-Walid ibn 'Abdul Malik, and it was through him that the final decisions were made concerning matters of state, legislation, the welfare of the people, and so on. In fact, any aspects of governance were referred to him by his regional governors when they were unsure. Because the Muslim world had become too vast to be overseen by one man, successive khalifas had appointed regional governors from the various countries to deal with matters of state on their behalves. Musa ibn Nusayr was one such governor, and it was his standard procedure to consult the Khalifa al-Walid.[7]

Having sent the letter to the *Amirul Mu'mineen*, the Commander of the Faithful, Musa waited patiently for an answer from Damascus. It was some weeks before the messenger returned amidst a chorus of trumpets and flying dust. Dismounting and brushing himself down, he hurried to

---

[7] The Khalifat no longer exists. Its physical authority was destroyed in 1924, aided by Western powers and secular movements in the Middle East. Many Muslims are still striving to re-establish it so that the Muslim World will be governed once again by one Khalifa.

the Governor's quarters, greeted his Commander-in-Chief with the customary '*as-salamu 'alaykum*' (peace be with you), and handed him the all-important letter bearing the Khalifa's seal. Having torn it open impatiently, Musa read the contents and it was as he had expected.

Khalifa al-Walid had sanctioned the expedition on the condition that Musa only make an initial incursion for the time being. He warned, "Do not under any condition expose large numbers of troops at present. Investigate the situation, and what this Count had told you, then report your findings to me". With the go-ahead from Damascus, the decision was finally taken to make the historic crossing into the Iberian Peninsula.

***

CHAPTER EIGHT

- Musa ibn Nusayr's Governorship -

Musa ibn Nusayr had become Governor of Ifriqiya shortly after 700 CE. No comprehensive account of Muslim Iberia can be given without a portrait of the illustrious man who had taken the initiative to conquer the country.

Although Musa had risen to great heights, his beginnings by contrast were extremely humble. Many years previously, during the period of Abu Bakr's Khalifat, the Muslims had, under the celebrated commander Khalid ibn al-Walid, conquered and defeated the Persian Empire. While conquering the region that is now modern Iraq, the troops came across a fort at 'Aynut Tamr in the western part of the empire. In this fort they found a school[8] where many young Arab boys were being raised as Christians and trained to become priests. The Muslims closed down this school and took the boys away to train them as apprentices instead. One of these boys was a young teenager called Nusayr, who was later to become the father of Musa. Nusayr came from the Lakhm tribe, the same tribe to place the Lakhmid dynasty upon the throne. He had been given special training as a warrior and bodyguard and eventually he had entered the personal services of Mu'awiya, the fifth Khalifa.

Nusayr eventually became the father of many sons, one of whom was Musa. Musa was born in 641 CE (19AH) and

---

[8] This was a monastic school run by Nestorian Christians – a branch of Christianity found in the Arab world.

grew up to be tall, strong, and very handsome. He was athletic by nature and a gifted sportsman. He also had a sharp wit and intelligence, which was matched by his ambition to succeed and make a name for himself. With this in mind he entered military service and became a good soldier, taking part in many battles.

The Muslims at that time had done most of their conquering by land, and so far had attempted little by sea. Mu'awiya was the first khalifa to undertake sea warfare, and had recognised the need for a strong navy to expand the Muslim lands. This navy was responsible for capturing Cyprus, an expedition in which Musa had taken part. His tenacity during the capture of the island had earned him many commendations and amongst the troops his name had soon become synonymous with bravery. His acclaimed military career was monumental in propelling him into the political arena, where he already had many friends and where he shone equally well. In 702 CE 'Abdul 'Aziz, the Governor of Egypt and a close personal friend of Musa, appointed him Governor of Ifriqiya.

The Berber Problem

Parts of North Africa, and especially among the many Berber tribes, were still resistant to the new religion of Islam and many had apostacised – that is, they had left Islam to follow another faith or to return to the traditions of their forefathers.

The Berbers – the original inhabitants of the region – were hardy and fiercely independent. Their culture, language and customs were quite different from those of the Arabs. However, like the Arabs, they were tribal in nature and each tribe gave precedence and loyalty to its kin – examples are the tribes of the Almoravids and the Baranis. Despite this, there were variations to be found among the populations from one region to another. Many berbers were farmers and shepherds in the mountain regions; others led nomadic lifestyles on the barren wastes bordering the Sahara Desert; and others were merchants based in small regional towns.

'Amr ibn al-'As had been the first Muslim conqueror to subdue the Berbers. After his death, a number of important figures arrived in North Africa to continue the expansionist programme he had started. The Muslims had a policy whereby after they had conquered a region, they would integrate the local community into the affairs of the state. They would give them important positions, as well as a share of all the pro-ceeds of wars, a stipulation laid down by the Prophet, and in the Quran, "And know that out of all the booty that ye may acquire (in war), a fifth share is assigned to Allah and to the messenger, and to near relatives, orphans, the needy and the wayfarer..." (Quran 8: 41)

When Hassan ibn Nu'man and Uqba ibn Nafi had conquered parts of North Africa, they had recognised the importance of this policy as it allowed conquered peoples in their own autonomy to become part of the new community order rather than exist as a defeated, demoralised nation. In addition, by recruiting large numbers of Berbers into the Muslim armies, loyalty was encouraged by giving them a share of the large booties that had characterised the earlier campaigns. In order to promote further a feeling of camaraderie, and to establish a sense of belonging, many Berbers were also given *wala'* positions, which meant that they were a 'right-hand man' or 'client' of a particular clansman. These various inducements helped the success of the early campaigns whereby the integration of local communities promoted harmony between the two societies and allowed for the fluid and smooth transition from paganism into Islam.

When Musa became the Governor he also continued this policy as it served the interests of the Muslims very well, was acceptable to all concerned, and at the same time facilitated many conversions to Islam. However, in all societies there will be elements of disturbance and trouble-making tendencies, and among the Berbers there was no exception. Certain tribes resisted vigorously, particularly the Baranis and Zannata tribes, and so Musa took it upon himself to convert them personally.

He proceeded to lead extensive campaigns against the Hawwara, Zannata and Kutama groups. After several months of campaigns they finally submitted and declared the *Shahadah*.

***

Naturally, with conquest comes booty. Prior to this no Muslim general had ever acquired so much from the proceeds of war. The prisoners of war alone numbered over 60,000 and all of them had to be fed and treated well. No families were to be split up, the good treatment of prisoners being an absolute must in Islamic Law. The Khalifa did not believe the letter he had received from Musa confirming that so many people had been captured until he had seen them with his own eyes.

These were the golden years of Musa's governorship. His leadership style, efficiency in times of war and peace, and his superb diplomacy won him admirers far and wide. Then, suddenly, the patronage he had enjoyed from 'Abdul 'Aziz, the man who had brought him to power, came to an end with the latter's death. However, Musa's fame as a wise governor had spread far by then and so not only did he retain his hold on Ifriqiya but was also made Governor of the Maghrib, an area which covered most of North Africa.

Here, campaigning continued and Musa had sent a number of his sons on expeditions, as well as an intrepid young Berber soldier called Tariq ibn Ziyad to lead an advance against the tribes of the High Atlas Mountains. Leaving Tariq in charge of this offensive, Musa then travelled on to Tangiers, which also became a Muslim city. He eventually gave Tariq command over Tangiers as well as over the Sous, an area now in the south of Morocco. Tariq took command of the area with approximately 30,000 troops made up of both Berbers and Arabs.

It is reported in the biographies on Musa ibn Nusayr that, having conquered North Africa, he then rode into the sea and said aloud on horseback:

"O Most Glorious Allah! Had not the waters prevented me from moving forward I would have carried on, so that those who lie on the other side of these mountainous waves could have known and glorified Thee and Thy Name!"

Religious Education of the Berbers

Musa, as the overall governor, did not forget his religious obligations to the people he had conquered. He ordered the construction of mosques and *madrasahs*, and ordered the *imams* to teach the Berbers about Islam. Interestingly enough, once the Berbers had been introduced to the scholarly and intellectual side of Islam, and once they had seen how balanced, harmonious and simple the religion really was, they never again left the fold.

The Compromise with Count Julian

As most of North Africa had now become Muslim, Musa decided to make a compromise with his old adversary, Count Julian. Julian had been living amongst the Berbers for many years and so Musa had allowed him to keep his fortified town of Ceuta. This, ironically enough, was a move that served the seasoned general well in the years to come when he became one of the most romantic figures of Muslim history with his historic conquest of the Iberian Peninsula.

***

CHAPTER NINE

- Tariq ibn Ziyad's Landing -

With al-Walid's sanction, Musa prepared for the forthcoming expedition with zeal and enthusiasm. He was a born leader and fighter and did not want to lose his chance to expand the Islamic Empire, while at the same time leaving a good impression of himself with the Khalifa. Having discussed his plans with Julian and agreed on a course of action, it was finally decided in the spring of 710 CE to send troops over. Musa decided to dispatch a young and intrepid officer called Tarif ibn Malik to make an initial reconnaissance mission along the Iberian coastline to see if Julian's account was accurate. Tarif left with four hundred foot soldiers and one hundred horsemen – all Berbers – in four ships that had been supplied by Julian.

It was a clear spring day when Tarif boarded his ship. Glancing heavenwards at the peaceful sky he said a *du'a* to Allah for the safe crossing of his men. Then, stepping aboard the ship with a sweep of his cloak, he took a deep breath and let the fresh sea air fill his lungs. Relaxed and feeling calm about the journey he gave the orders for the release of the boat. The blustering winds made nearby seagulls fly off-course, whilst billowing up the sails ready for the departure. With the raising of the boat sails they were away. Waving farewell to Musa, who stood at the pier, the strong winds helped the boats glide out of the harbour as they sailed off into the open sea.

A little over an hour later they could see land on the horizon. There lay a world vastly different from the one that these soldiers had known so far. Two continents could not have been more different in outlook, custom and religion. The crossing had only taken a short time, but the gulf between the two worlds was much wider. As they sailed closer, the soldiers rushed to the deck to see the small white sun-baked houses scattered along the hillside, still a distinctive feature of modern Andalusia. Shepherds were gathering their flocks in as dusk fell, and young mothers were beckoning in their children playing outside. From the distance all looked peaceful and untroubled – people going about their lives as they had done for centuries, unaware that a new storm was brewing.

As they approached the shore, the Muslims decided to land on a small promontory at the southern-most tip of the European continent. This section of land has since borne Tarif's name. It became known as '*Jaziratu-t Tarif*', or 'Tarif's Headland', and is now the modern town of Tarifa.

Having rested, the Muslim soldiers spent the next few weeks scouring the local area to verify Julian's story. Having completed their expedition, they returned to North Africa in July of the same year and were able to confirm that the country did in fact appear to be defenceless and that it could be taken easily with Julian's assistance.

Report Back to Musa

However, on hearing Tarif's report, Musa was still not convinced that he should risk the whole of his army. Nevertheless, encouraged by his subordinate's success and hearing that Roderick was otherwise engaged quelling an uprising of Basques in the north, he arranged for another expedition the following year.

In 711CE, during the auspicious Muslim month of Rajab, he dispatched his trusted governor Tariq with a troop of 7,000 Berber soldiers. They again sailed in the ships provided by Julian and landed this time on a mighty rock on the other side of the bay from *Jaziratu-t Tarif*. This second promontory has since been immortalised by history with the name '*Jabalu-t Tariq*' – 'The Mountain of Tariq', nowadays called Gibraltar.

At the foot of this mountain lay the town of Cartaya (now long-gone), which the Muslims captured and used as a base for their headquarters. Having fortified the area, the Muslims marched on further and captured the town of Algeciras, on the tip of the Peninsula.

General Theodemir had been left to defend it on Roderick's behalf but it fell easily. The terror-struck general wrote to Roderick:

"My Lord, there have come forces averse to us from different quarters. Whether they have dropped from heaven, or sprung up through the earth, I know not, having found them suddenly before me. I resisted them with all my power, but have been compelled to yield to the impetuosity of their attacks."

Tariq then moved inland meeting little or no resistance on the way. Encouraged by this fact, and seeing how badly defended the country really was, he went even further inland until he reached a large wetland called Laguna de Janda. While here he heard that Roderick, alarmed by the news that he had received, was hurriedly marching south at the head of a huge army.

News soon spread through the ranks of Tariq's army that the

Visigoths had an estimated 100,000 men, while the Muslims numbered only a few thousand. Rumblings of alarm spread through the camps as the Berbers wondered how they could tackle such a mighty force without being annihilated. Tariq, meanwhile, had none of the misgivings of his troops. Fuelled with religious zeal and thinking only of Allah Almighty, he thought of himself as a soldier of Islam. Nevertheless, sensing that his men were growing nervous at the impending fight, very cleverly he decided to burn the four boats that had carried them across. Hence there was no possible way of going back. He then remembered a passage from the Quran:

"O ye who believe! When ye meet a force be firm, and call Allah in remembrance much that ye may prosper. And obey Allah and His messenger, and fall into no disputes, lest ye lose heart and your power depart; and be patient and persevering: for Allah is with those who patiently persevere." (Quran 8: 45-46)

Re-invigorated by his religious inspirations, he made one of the most memorable speeches in Islamic military history, which one chronicler has preserved in this way:

"Friends! The fathomless deep is raging behind, we cannot return to our mother country. If to the eternal disgrace of our country, Islam and race, we turn our backs like cowards, we can only be devoured by the yawning waves. Put far from you the disgrace from which you flee in dreams and attack this monarch who has left his strongly fortified city to meet you.

"Here is a splendid opportunity to defeat him if you will consent to expose yourself freely to death. Do not believe that I desire to incite you to face dangers, which I shall refuse to share with you. If we go forward as the worthy sons of our mothers and bravely attack the enemies, we can either defeat them and earn eternal laurels on this earth, or we can lay down our lives on a field of undying glory and martyrdom. Remember that if you suffer a few moments in patience, you will afterwards enjoy supreme delight. Do not imagine that your fate can be separated from mine and rest assured that if you fall, I shall perish with you or avenge you. I hereby unsheath my sword and go forward; tell me, how many of you are prepared to follow me?"

Swirling around, his cloak dancing in the warm afternoon breeze, he carefully watched the expressions on his men's faces. He was not to be disappointed. A look of appeasement and renewed vigour shone on each man's face. Some saw visions of Paradise before them, while others were overwhelmed by the smell of victory.

So, armed with an additional 5,000 men sent as reinforcements by Musa, and with one resounding cry of "Allahu Akbar!", they marched out to meet their foe.

***

CHAPTER TEN

- Tariq Defeats Roderick -

The battle that was to ensue was so significant that it has been listed as one of the twenty most decisive battles in the history of the world. In realistic terms it is doubtful whether Tariq would have won with so few soldiers on his side. However, fired with religious fervour and a need to serve Allah, he ignited the enthusiasm of his soldiers with his rousing speech. In addition, Tariq had the party of Julian and Witiza's disaffected family on his side.

Roderick tried to appeal to them by stating that all of Christendom was at stake and that therefore the nobles allied to Witiza's family should reconcile their differences with him and fight against a common foe. However, his treachery of the past was not so readily forgotten. Moreover, his own noblemen had good cause to doubt that he would listen to their grievances should he win the battle, and although legally bound to honour their king, privately they had decided to side with the opposition.

The two armies met on the banks of a river called Wadi Bekka, southeast of Medina Sidonia in the South on 20 July 711CE. The battle lasted for almost a week, but ultimately the Muslims gained the upper hand as the treachery and betrayal of their Spanish allies came to their assistance.

Witiza's two sons led the two wings of the Hispano-Visigothic army. This was mainly made up of a motley crew of badly trained serfs and slaves, who were only too ready to desert

King Roderick given the opportunity. Bishop Oppas, King Egica's son and Witiza's brother, led another contingent. At a critical juncture during the battle when the signal was given, they were to desert the King and side with the opposition. Roderick, oblivious of the conspiracy against him, arrived on the battlefield shaded by a magnificent canopy and bedecked in his shining armour. He was to lead the centre.

It was a blisteringly hot day for the first engagement. As the two parties lunged towards each other, the battlefield erupted with the clang of armour and the flashing of drawn swords. Resounding cries of "Allahu Akbar!" could be heard as troops rushed forward, colliding into the opposition who were armed with battle-axes and maces. The beat of a hundred drums thumped and echoed in their hearts, giving them the rhythm needed to co-ordinate their marching feet. As one contingent fell another took its place. Horses reared up in the flying dust and careered into each other. Blood and dismembered limbs could be seen hacked from their owners as cries of agony littered the air and stilled the heart.

The Cross was battered and flung down. Attempts were made by Christian soldiers on their steeds to lift it up, but it became trampled underfoot. All around hails of arrows sailed through the air, lodging into their victims' arms, legs and throats. Tariq's men staggered forward, fighting bravely among shouts of valour mixed with the groans of death.

In the midst of all the chaos, the party loyal to Witiza broke free and, much to the disbelief of Roderick's squadron, took up the banner of the Muslims. Both sides pressed on. Roderick's contingent was well equipped and managed to withstand the Muslims for a while, but then Tariq came to the forefront and took up the fight against Roderick's personal defences.

He headed the last charge and fought so vigorously that the enemies were utterly routed. Turning to survey the carnage, he spotted Roderick's white steed, Orelia, galloping wildly across the battlefield without her rider. Attempts were made to locate the King but by the evening of the last day of the battle, he had still not been found. The next morning, Roderick's slippers were found by the river but his body was missing never to be seen again. In all probability he had drowned and was washed out to sea – a sad ending for a king who never fully realised how his countrymen had betrayed him.

With the death of Roderick, the Muslims had effectively won a spectacular victory. Without a king at the head of state, Roderick's kingdom was very vulnerable, and Tariq fully realised this. Musa had instructed him to withdraw and return to North Africa but Tariq, grasping the enormity of the opportunity, decided to push on. He was aware of the duplicity of the local noblemen and realised that this was a chance to take advantage of the region's crumbling political climate. So, in defiance of his governor, he marched on.

***

CHAPTER ELEVEN

- The March to Cordoba -

Tariq rode at the head of an army full of the confidence and enthusiasm that comes with victory. Spirits were high and morale was boosted further by the obvious fact that the Muslims, much to their surprise, were perceived as liberators by many sections of Hispano-Visigothic society. The disaffected flocked to their side and disposal. The poorer classes applauded the Muslims as they passed them in the countryside while the Jews, who had for so long suffered under the yoke of oppression, facilitated the conquerors with their help and assistance.

Most cities and towns had few standing armies to defend them and so resistance was futile. Tariq divided his forces into three sections and sent them in three different directions. One contingent marched on Malaga towards the east; the second towards Cordoba, and the third to Granada. Tariq himself then made his memorable march on Toledo in the central Iberian region.

All around them confusion and terror reigned. "Allah", said one Arab chronicler, "had filled the hearts of the infidels with terror". It was true. The Visigoth nobility, fearful for their lives, ran riotously through the streets. They had never before seen such strange looking horsemen, dressed in white with large turbans on their heads, carrying scimitars. They rode in a long disciplined line with pride, carrying a standard bearing Arabic writing and professing Islam as their religion. People stared at them in the streets, sometimes from behind half-closed shutters, sometimes from the pavement itself.

The March Continues

Swiftly, and with tremendous speed, Tariq's troops moved from town to town. At Sidonia and Carmona the invaders were actually invited in. At Ecija – to where knights from the remnants of Roderick's beleaguered army had fled – attempts at resistance were made but, after the Muslims had offered reasonable terms, they surrendered.

Tariq had in the meantime marched on Toledo, the Visigothic capital. Here indescribable chaos reigned. The wealthy of the surrounding towns had rushed to Toledo hoping to get sanctuary with the Bishop in his church. However, Bishop Sindered, to his eternal disgrace, had lost his nerve and deserted his flock to flee to Rome. In his wake, much of the city's nobility followed and so all that remained were the serfs, slaves and the traitors who had aided the Muslims, such as Witiza's family and Count Julian.

Witiza's relatives asked to be rewarded for their part in the campaigns and were duly given 3,000 farms – part of the crown lands – while Bishop Oppas was made Governor of Toledo and henceforth was responsible for collecting the *Jizya,* or tax, from the people.

Archidona, which lies just north of Malaga and to the west of Granada was next on the path of the conquerors and was captured without a single blow as the inhabitants had fled to the mountains. Malaga was also easy prey and capitulated, while the town of Elvira – a site near to Granada - surrendered and was garrisoned by a mixture of Jews and Muslims to prevent it from being recaptured.

The Fall of Cordoba

Cordoba, which was to become the official capital of Islamic Iberia – soon to be called 'Al-Andalus' or 'Andalus' – was delivered into Muslim hands by a shepherd who had shown the Berbers a breach in the city's boundary wall. The city was already in a decrepit condition because the Roman bridge linking it to the surrounding countryside was damaged. And so, a soldier was directed through a huge hole in the rampart by Mughith, a Greek officer dispatched to capture the city. Once in, during the still of night, the soldier unwrapped his turban and threw it back through the hole down to his companions below. They stealthily climbed through the breach and then overpowered the guards at the city's gate. The garrison, realising what had happened and terrified for their lives, ran for cover to a nearby convent where they took refuge for the next three months. When they finally emerged they saw that the city had been taken. It had been left in charge of the Jews. They were to look after the administration and running of the city while the Berbers moved further inland to see what more could be captured.

As Stanley Lane-Poole pointed out in 1887 in his book *The Moors in Spain*:

"Cordova was left in the keeping of the Jews, who had proved themselves staunch allies of the Moslems in the campaign and who ever afterwards enjoyed great consideration at the hands of the conquerors. The Moors admitted them into their intimacy... Wherever the arms of the Saracens penetrated, there we shall always find the Jews in close pursuit: while the Arabs fought, the Jew trafficked and when the fighting was over, Jew and Moor and Persian joined in that cultivation of learning and philosophy, arts and sciences, which pre-eminently distinguished the rule of the Saracens in the Middle Ages."

Tariq's troops continued to travel eastwards until they reached a mountain pass called Murcia, which guarded the district of the same name. A Visigoth governor called Theodemir had been left in charge of the pass, which formed a superb natural barrier protecting the eastern seaboard. On hearing of the Muslims' approach, he defended it admirably for a while by using guerrilla warfare. If it were lost it would mean that the Berbers could then capture the whole of the eastern part of the Peninsula.

The Muslims had realised this and made an all-out concerted effort to capture Theodemir and his men. Realising that guerrilla warfare was very hard to combat, the Muslim Captain challenged Theodemir to an open battle by taunting him that he could not possibly win. Theodemir foolishly took the bait and his entire force went out to meet the Muslims. They were subsequently massacred on the plains near the mountains. Theodemir escaped with his trusted page and fled for the city of Orihuela on the borders of the Mediterranean Sea.

Having reached there, he heard that the Muslims were in hot pursuit. Orihuela, like most of the South, was badly defended. Theodemir saw there were hardly any military men left as most of them had fallen in the field. Out of desperation he persuaded the women of the city to dress up as men and wrap their long hair around the bottom half of their faces so that they looked like beards. Then, arming them with spears and lances, he made them stand as sentries around the walls of the city. When the Muslim Captain arrived, he was surprised to find the city so well defended. "Know this," stated the intrepid governor when he went out to meet the opposition with a flag of truce in his hand, "You can see that the city is well-defended and can withstand a long siege. However, our Prince is desirous to make peace. If you promise to allow the inhabitants to go free with their goods and lives intact, we are willing to surrender. If not we are prepared to undertake a long campaign against you."

The Muslim captain agreed to the terms and the papers were drawn up. Once they had been sealed it was decided to wait until the following morning to let the inhabitants go. At dawn, a great procession issued forth. The Muslims waited to see the men, but all that came stumbling out was Theodemir and his faithful page in their battered armour, followed by an endless assortment of women, children and old men.

"But where are the soldiers we saw last night?" cried the perplexed captain. "What soldiers?" exclaimed Theodemir. "We have none, all you saw last night were these women dressed as men!" So amused was the captain by the clever trick that was played on him that he decided to reward Theodemir there and then for his shrewdness.

He was made Governor of Murcia, and his community allowed the freedom to practise Christianity. This was on the condition that each year a tribute was paid to the conquerors in the form of wheat, grape juice, vinegar and other foodstuffs, together with payment of the *Jizya*, or personal tax, which was paid by non-Muslims to receive protection from their conquerors. As a result, the district of Murcia was for centuries afterwards known to the Muslims as Tudmir, or the 'land of Theodemir'.

How the Conquest was achieved

What had started out as a foray had, by the end of 711 CE, ended in the surrender of a large part of the Southern Iberian region. Chroniclers in the years to come were at great pains to explain and justify how God could have allowed this to happen to a Christian kingdom. Most medieval commentators confirmed that there were a number of reasons for the disaster. Amongst the most obvious was the immorality of the Visigothic Kings. King Witiza, we are told "taught all Spain to sin". He had a number of mistresses and many wives as well, not something tolerated by the Catholic Church. He had even encouraged his priests to marry, which was against Catholic Canon Law.

Later historians have cited political decay and the injustices of the social system as reasons that allowed a foreign nation to capture part of the country so easily. In addition, the treachery of Witiza's family and Count Julian had aided the foreigners. For the Muslims, however, there was but one simple explanation: Allah Almighty had willed it. It was in Allah's Good Grace that this kingdom had fallen, and it was His decision to allow the enlightened administration of the Muslims to flourish in these lands for the next eight hundred years.

***

Chapter Twelve

- Musa Arrives -

It was not long before Musa had heard of the phenomenal successes of his lieutenant. Fired with enthusiasm and wanting to participate in the action, he too decided to cross into the Iberian Peninsula hot on the heels of his subordinate. He arrived the following year, in June 712 CE, with 18,000 Syrian and other Arabian troops. Amongst his crew were many descendants of the Companions (*Sahabah*) of the Prophet.

He decided to avoid the route taken by Tariq and instead concentrated his attention on the western seaboard. He took Medina Sidonia and Carmona in succession. Carmona, interestingly enough, was handed over to him by the local inhabitants themselves. A number of men had pretended to be fugitives on the run from the Muslims and had pounded on the city's doors in the dead of the night, begging to be allowed in. Having gained access to the city, they opened the doors to the Arabs.

Seville, which was the cultural heartland of the region and was at one time the Roman capital, put up a brave fight for many months before finally capitulating.

Musa then marched on Merida, which was the most difficult city to capture. Here there was intense fighting that dragged on for a year. Finally, the Muslim garrison employed siege engines to bombard and pound the city into submission, which it did in July 713 CE. Musa then marched towards Toledo, where Tariq had made his headquarters. It was here that Tariq, on hearing that his commander was about to arrive, made elaborate preparations to welcome him.

On the day of Musa's arrival, Tariq had dismounted from his horse and walked forward, humbly extending his hand to his leader in welcome, saying, "I am merely your assistant; this conquest is yours".

However, he was greeted with a whip, lashed across his face by Musa. The spirited general erupted in anger and cried, "I told you to only make a foray, and then immediately return to Africa! What possessed you to march on the whole of the Peninsula?"

Tariq, unperturbed by the insult, explained his motives. After a while, the two were happily reconciled. Their joint forces then moved on to Aragon in the north of the country, and then to Leon and Astoria. Barcelona opened its gates, as did a number of other cities. Without a proper leader to co-ordinate a defence the country was powerless, and as no leader came forward, the Muslim conquest amounted to a promenade – in fewer than three years most of the region had fallen to Musa.

His later successors carried on his strategies and the entire region that is now modern Spain was conquered in just over six years. The area now known as Portugal was captured a few years later and was named 'al-Gharb', meaning 'the Western [Province]', and this is from where the modern region of the 'Algarve' takes its name.

Only a small mountain stronghold held out in the Asturias in the North of the country, made up of an ethnic mix of some 30 men and 10 women under the leadership of Pelayo. However, the uncharacteristically short sighted Musa dismissed them with contempt, feeling that they could be tackled later, and he then moved on towards what is now France.

By this time inflammatory propaganda had swept across the border. The Franks[9] knew only too well what had happened in the Iberian Peninsula and were watching their borders nervously, wondering when the invasion of their country was to take place. Defeatist sentiments had already spread like wildfire, together with sensationalist stories about how the Muslims had murdered, raped, pillaged and massacred in their wake. Most of this was conspiratorial in nature. Rumour after rumour circulated about this unknown race and religion that conquered only at the point of a sword. People threw up their arms in terror, not knowing what to do or where to run.

In fact, few atrocities had taken place; Musa would not have allowed it. If they did, they were severely condemned as they went against the doctrines of the faith. Musa was a religious man, and he knew that he was answerable to Allah Almighty for all of his actions, including the commands he gave to his soldiers.

"O ye that believe! Betray not the trust of Allah and the messenger, nor misappropriate knowingly things entrusted to you." (Quran 8:27)

In addition, he was a military man and military conquest was his primary concern.

"Against them make ready your strength to the utmost of your power, including steeds of war, to strike terror into the hearts

---

[9] The contemporary dynasty and inhabitants of what is now France.

of the enemies… Whatever ye shall spend in the cause of Allah shall be repaid unto you, and ye shall not be treated unjustly." (Quran 8:60)

***

Musa defeated Languedoc, but advanced no further east than Frejus. Then, standing on the Pyrenees Mountains, he looked out across the vast expanse of beautiful land: the deep valleys, the pulsating river, the clean air; and contemplated conquering the whole of Europe. No doubt the intrepid viceroy could have done it. There was no leader of any magnitude to resist him and there was no unity between the European countries – which more often than not were fighting each other – to hinder his progress. A momentous opportunity lay in his hands for the future of Europe; the continent could have been at his feet. What a service to Islam and what a duty to Allah would have been achieved if he had been able to invite almost the rest of the known world to Islam. It seemed that there was no one to stop him.

However, as fate would have it, it was a fellow Muslim and not a Christian who halted his progress. As Europe quivered on the brink of a possible religious revolution, Musa was ordered to push on no further. The timid, and perhaps short sighted, policy of the Khalifa's administration would not allow Musa to advance and he was told to withdraw. If the cautionary foreign policy of Damascus had not recalled him at this time, who knows what would have been the condition of Europe today. It could have been absorbing the melodious recitation of the Glorious Quran on Fridays, instead of observing its empty churches on Sundays. A wonderful opportunity was lost forever, never again to be repeated.

In fact, although Musa had been forced to abandon his scheme, shortly afterwards in 719 CE another Muslim general took up the mantle and occupied southern France by capturing the cities of Narbonne and Carcassonne. Having fortified his position there, he was joined by 'Anbasah ibn Suhaym, who had moved as far north as Burgundy and Aquitania. He was supported in the west by 'Abdu-r Rahman al-Ghafiqi, who had victoriously defeated the Franks at Toulouse, and then moved on to sack Bordeaux. By 732CE he had reached Tours, which is just south-west of Paris. It was at Tours, considered to be the religious capital of Gaul that the Franks finally realised that they would soon go the way of their Iberian neighbours unless action was taken immediately. A young man called Charles, son of Pepin Heristal, who had been 'Mayor of the Palace' of the Merovingian-Frankish[10] Royal Court, was appointed to deal with the situation.

In the words of an unknown Arab chronicler:

"The Muslims smote their enemies and passed the River Garonne and laid waste to the country and took captives without number. Their armies went through all the places like a desolating storm. Prosperity made those warriors insatiable. At the passage of the river, 'Abdu-r Rahman overthrew the Count, and the Count retired to his stronghold, but the Muslims fought against it and entered it by force and slew the Count; for everything gave way to their scimitars, which were the robbers of lives. All the nations of the Franks trembled at that terrible army and they betook them to their King Caldus (Charles Martel) and told him of the havoc by the Muslim horsemen, and how they rode at their will through all the land

[10] This is the dynasty that ruled over this region at this time. 'France' did not become 'French' until much later.

of Narbonne, Toulouse and Bordeaux. They told the King of the death of their Count. Then the King bade them be of good cheer and offered to aid them..."

Charles met the Muslims for battle at Tours (Poitiers) in October 732 CE. The Muslims rejoiced at the prospect of another victory, their success so far unchecked. However, Charles and his men were of better calibre and as soldiers they were as hardy as their Muslim counterparts. Vigorous and bred to arms since childhood, they lived and died by the sword and relished a fight with any adversary. Had the Muslims won this battle there is no reason to suppose they would have stopped there; they could have carried on up to the northern territories.

However, Charles and his steadfast men fought vigorously for six days. Aided by the cold drizzly weather, which facilitated their cause, the Franks wielded their maces and swords with insuperable force. By the fifth day, the stamina of the Muslims was waning but, faithful to their commander, they fought on. Despite this, by the end of the week it was obvious that they would lose. Charles's men cut them down with an almost impregnable might, crushing the force out of them. So badly overwhelmed were the Muslims that, right up to this day, the battle site has been sorrowfully called, 'The Pavement of Martyrs'.

Medieval chroniclers often retell this battle as being 'the one that saved Europe'. Its events led to the historian Gibbon's famous piece[11] on the prospect of having minarets instead of spires on the skylines of Oxford and Cambridge, and mosques

---

[11] Gibbon, Edward, *The History of the Decline and Fall of the Roman Empire*, published originally in six volumes from 1776-1788.

in London instead of the cathedrals and churches.

Europe breathed a sigh of relief and applause was audible all around as danger had been avoided for the moment. A limit had been set on the Muslims' progress and their shattering defeat meant that henceforth the Christians affectionately called Charles Martel, 'Charles the Hammer'. This battle had convinced the Muslims never again to attempt a conquest of the Frankish territories for all the years that they remained in the Iberian lands. Historians, such as Rheinhart Dozy[12], have likewise cited this battle as marking the end of the great Muslim expansionist programme that had started shortly after the Prophet's ﷺ death almost one hundred years previously.

The Iberian episode had marked the closing chapter of the early campaigns. Here the line was drawn and, recognising this as a sign from the Almighty, they decided to stop. Henceforth from 732 CE the Muslims decided, for the time being, to consolidate and to organise their territories in the West, and their inhabitants, rather than to continue the search for new lands.

***

[12] Dozy, Rheinhart, *Muslims in Spain*, Darf Publishing, London, 1988.

CHAPTER THIRTEEN

- A Period of Consolidation -

Musa could not disobey the direct command of the Khalifa in Damascus, who was telling him to withdraw. Therefore, he decided to consolidate his position in the north instead.

He captured Galicia and drove the mountain people deeper into the rocky Cantabrian Mountains. Here, near the Picos de Europa, they waged guerrilla warfare. However, covered on all sides by Musa and his armies, one by one they surrendered until only a single leader Pelayo – perhaps a Visigothic lord – remained with few supporters. He fought vigorously but eventually was hemmed in on all sides. It was only a matter of time before his provisions would run out and he too would have to surrender. However, intervention from Damascus yet again prevented Musa from crushing this resistance. Musa and Tariq were summoned for immediate recall to Damascus.

Return to Damascus

One is tempted to ask how the Khalifa al-Walid could have made such a disastrous decision. He had been kept well informed about the conquests and the huge gains for Islam, both in monetary and territorial terms. By allowing this small resistance to remain, given time, they swelled in numbers and offered an effective fighting force against the Muslims. It was from the north in the years to come that armies eventually rose up to defeat and expel the Muslims from Andalus. Musa, able to do nothing and leaving Pelayo and his small fighting force as a minor irritation to be dealt with later, travelled south to organise the government of the rest of the country.

Musa returned to Cordoba and established it as the capital of Andalus. Control of the capital was essential, as it was from here that all legislative and political decisions were made. It is not understood why Cordoba was chosen as it had not been either the Roman or the Visigoth capital. However, it did have an important strategic value, and this may have been the overriding factor.

On all sides it linked to the surrounding countryside. To the north lay the Sierra Morena mountain range, which meant that it was well protected from marauding bandits; while to the west lay Seville with easy access to the Guadiana and Guadalquivir rivers. In addition, Cordoba bordered the fertile plains of the south, where a rich agricultural hinterland had been established for many years. However, the most important reason of all could have been the fact that the city was relatively empty and that therefore many different Arab tribes could settle there together, including the Lakhm and Judham tribes. This would not have been possible in the old Roman capital of Seville, or the former Visigoth capital of Toledo, where the existing populations still remained in large numbers.

Musa decided to appoint his second son, 'Abdu-l 'Aziz, as Viceroy and it was he who later set up his government in Seville. Under him ruled the *Hajib*, or 'Chamberlain', who dispensed his proclamations to his various viziers. It was a highly structured and organised system of government that had officials filtering down to all levels. There existed a Chief-of-Police, market inspectors, librarians and tax inspectors.

Another son was left in charge of guarding the coastline and the Navy, while the rest of the Municipal Government was made up of men of Berber, Celt-Iberian and Arab origins.

Why the Muslims were so successful

The reasons for the smooth passage of the Muslims into Iberian culture, without much hostility from the vanquished, have been much debated by scholars throughout history. The reasons are numerous and manifold but, undoubtedly, a major factor facilitating their position has to have been their charitable and philanthropic outlook.

To their credit, they were very reasonable and generous in their terms of surrender. Many of the inhabitants had braced themselves for another wave of unpleasant butchery and carnage, but were happily surprised when instead they were offered liberal terms, which made yielding more palatable.

The first thing that the Muslims did was to set about the huge task of completely re-organising the country and re-populating the cities. They decided to break down the political and social systems that had been institutionalised for generations. This was achieved by smashing the power of the aristocracy and the clergy by stripping them of their land and re-distributing it more fairly amongst the population.

Previously, the servile classes had had no rights over the land they tilled. The Muslims, however, made them tenant farmers, which meant they could keep a part of the crops they produced provided they gave a share of it to their Muslim landlord. This proved to be a great incentive to small farmers and was part of the reason why agriculture began to flourish widely for the first time in the region.For the conquerors, this served two purposes. Firstly, it allowed for the smooth absorption of their society into that of the Visigoths – by being munificent to the farmers they did not have to face the customary hostility that comes with a take-over. Secondly, it allowed the host nation to continue its natural economic industry – the conquerors were unaccustomed to labouring in the fields, but the Iberian peasants proved willing to do it for them.

Although the aristocracy had lost much of their lands, there were still plenty of Christian overlords who owned expansive estates. These landlords were now wary of treating their slaves badly, because any complaint from them – or better still if the slaves had declared the *Shahadah* and become instant Muslims – and they would be answerable to the Arabs. In fact, the slaves, having seen no hope of deliverance under the previous regimes, began to convert to Islam in droves because, in so doing, they also became free and stood equal to all men.

Not all the land was confiscated from the nobility. For instance, there were many people in the Ebro Valley who were allowed to retain their properties. The goodwill shown to them was paid back to the Muslims, with time, as a fair number later converted to Islam. Among these were the Banu Qasi of Tudela and the Banu Amrus of Huesca.

***

CHAPTER FOURTEEN

- Establishing Al-Andalus -

The Muslims decided to divide the Peninsula into four large regions. Each had its own governor who in turn was answerable to the overall Viceroy. The conquerors also allowed many of the cities within these provinces to run themselves. The first province included the cities of Granada and Cordoba. The second covered the middle part of Spain and included the cities of Madrid and Valencia. The third spread out to the west and incorporated parts of present day Portugal, as well as the city of Salamanca; while the fourth was in the north of the country and included Barcelona and Tortosa.

Meanwhile, different Arab and Berber groups had rapidly crossed the border in the wake of the invasion, and settled over a wide and diversified geographical area. People had come from Egypt, Mesopotamia, Syria and the wider Levantine region. They mingled together as one brotherhood and jointly made their way to the mosques that were springing up to accommodate the growing population, which, including the original inhabitants, stood at approximately 4-6 million. In fact, by the end of the tenth century, Cordoba's population stood at about 250,000; Granada's at 26,000 and Toledo's at about 38,000. The combined industry of these people, and the skills they brought with them, turned Andalus into a garden.

As Syed Amir 'Ali wrote in 1928:

"The Saracen settlers came chiefly from countries which were essentially agricultural such as Egypt, Syria and Persia. They were endowed like the Jews, who followed them in all their colonies, with the commercial instinct, and were led towards industry by the teachings of the Prophet, which made labour a religious duty. They accordingly took in hand with unequalled energy the material development of Spain, which had hitherto lain sterile under the Christian government. They introduced various agronomic works; they fertilised the uncultivated lands, repopulated the cities that were deserted, ornamented them with beautiful monuments and united them by a number of industrial and commercial ties. They gave to the people a right, which had never been permitted to them by the Gothic kings, the right of alienating their lands. Spain, emancipated from feudal servitude which had hung so long like a curse on the land, became the most populous and most industrious of European countries. The Arabs turned Spain into a garden; they organised a model administration and gave impetus to the arts and sciences."

The first Viceroy, as already mentioned, was Musa's son 'Abdul 'Aziz. He had married Roderick's widow, Egilona, who the Muslims called Umm 'Asim. He set up a *diwan*, an administrative body, which was to oversee the implementation of Islamic law in the country. He was considered by some to be a benevolent and wise leader and, through his tact and conciliatory methods, he managed to unite and hold the country together.[13]

He also encouraged inter-racial marriage and this is another reason why the integration of the Muslims into indigenous

---

[13] Some historians, such as Prof. T. B. Irving, blame his marriage to the fanatical Catholic Egilona for forcing him into more and more compromising positions during the course of his governorship.

society succeeded to such a degree. As the North Africans and Arabs mixed with the native community they not only adopted a number of the local customs that were permissible within the bounds of Islam, but also saw this as an opportunity for spreading the faith through the system of inter-marriage.

Many ladies from the leading nobility married into Arab families, such as Sara, the granddaughter of Witiza, who had married two Arab husbands in succession. It was also from her family that the famous tenth century historian Ibn al-Quttiyah was descended. The involvement of such important sections of the Visigothic nobility in the affairs of the Muslims most definitely accounts for some of the lack of opposition.

Even the clergy, always the ones to cause the greatest outcry where a change of power was concerned, were not scandalised by the alliance of their former queen with a Muslim. The Bishop of Beja even stated that he regarded such a thing "to be quite normal".

Why the inhabitants converted to Islam

There is a line in the Quran that states, "Let there be no compulsion in religion, truth will shine out from error".[14] Muslims are told to offer *da'wah* to others, in other words to 'invite' newcomers to the faith, but then to allow them to draw their own conclusions. Forced conversions are not permissible; people should have the right to choose.

As the inhabitants observed their new society and the customs

---

[14] Quran 2:256.

that the Arabs introduced, many were drawn towards the obvious comradeship and co-operation between the Muslims. The luckless peasants, who until then had had a worthless existence together with the impoverished Middle Classes, noticed that even the humblest Muslim had a sense of pride and belonging as part of a bigger religious community. Islam saw slavery in a very different light from Christianity.

The Prophet ﷺ had stipulated that many sins could be expiated through the emancipation of another human soul and so many slaves felt encouraged to convert. No doubt there were some who converted simply to win their freedom, while others genuinely marvelled at the simplicity of the faith, and others may have converted because Islam presented an alternative to Christianity.

It must be remembered that Catholicism was still relatively new to the Iberian Peninsula and in many cases most people simply paid lip service to the faith, as they had received no real religious education. Their understanding of Catholicism was rudimentary since the new faith and 'paganism'[15] were still competing with each other in terms of their numbers of worshippers. In fact, at the time of the Visigoth invasion, Catholicism was not deeply rooted in the local society and the country still had large pagan populations which continued to adhere to their ancient cults.

The region had remained shackled to its former deities, the fetters from which it could not shake itself free. The

[15] It is possible that the 'paganism' referred to was simply a dismissive term used by the Catholic Church to define the Arian Christians of the region, who they did not recognise as being 'real Christians'.

implementations of Constantine's edicts had been slow in passing through to all areas of the Roman Empire. So, when the Muslims offered an alternative form of salvation, many leapt at the chance as it guaranteed their freedom while adding to the cohesion between the two cultures.

The treatment of minority faiths

In matters of faith the downtrodden and beleaguered Jews were also allowed – finally – to follow Mosaic Laws without impediment, whilst those that chose to remain Christians found that they too were unhindered in matters of faith. People could also appoint their own judges to oversee religious proclamations. Christian laws often differed from Islamic ones and so the towns choosing to remain Christian retained their own laws, judges and administrators.

No one was persecuted because of his or her faith, and there were no forced conversions. A person could remain Jewish, Muslim or Christian. The different religious groups even had governors of their choice to collect taxes on their behalf and these were then entrusted to the Muslims to deposit in the Treasury, known as the *Baytu-l Mal*. As a result, the majority of Jews and Christians lost next to nothing.

All the offices of Local Government, and to some extent those of the National Government, were open to anyone. Appointments were based on merit, and not on colour or creed. Many present-day regimes, who constantly criticise the Muslims for their way of life, would do well to examine the truth about how these past societies were governed.

Taxation Reforms

The heavy taxes that had ruined industry and burdened the Middle Classes were removed, and an altogether more practical and intelligible tax system was introduced based on Quranic laws.

Revenue for the upkeep of the State – which was later spent on public works like street lighting, public baths and libraries – was collected by way of a number of means, including the *Jizya* and the *Kharaj*.

The *Jizya,* or 'poll tax', was payable by non-Muslims because it was in lieu of military service, which they were not obligated to do, and it went towards the defence of the realm. A rich man would pay 48 dirhams per year; the Middle Classes 24 dirhams, and the poor 12 dirhams. This was not necessarily payable in one go but depended on circumstances, and could be paid in instalments over a 12-month period. In addition, the blind, the sick, women, children, and those leading a monastic lifestyle, were exempt.

The *Kharaj,* or 'land tax', was payable by Muslims and non-Muslims alike if they owned land. The amount varied according to the type of soil and so, for instance, different amounts were due on clay or sandy soil. The tax also varied according to the productive capacity of the land. Hence, if there was a poor harvest for a given year, the tax could be waived.

The Military

Even with such equitable terms the Muslims still realised that it would be wise to keep some form of standing army. There was always the chance of minor incursions from the north, and also the possibility of invasion from other countries in Europe. To avoid the risk of such confrontations – or at least to keep them at bay – a military presence was established. The Army was made up either of volunteers or of trained soldiers who had been brought from other Muslim countries on a contractual basis. Each division, or '*jund*', as they were called, comprised of soldiers from a particular country to aid the cohesion within a given contingent. These were then deployed to areas deemed vulnerable, such as the border crossings and the seaports. They were astonishingly mobile and well disciplined and could be organised in a hurry should an emergency arise.

***

Hence, there arose in Andalus a new society based on Allah Almighty's laws, and it was entirely different from anything that the host nation had seen before. As a result, many of the inhabitants preferred the rule of the Muslims to their former masters.

***

Chapter Fifteen

- Musa Returns to Damascus -

Having consolidated the administration in Andalus and ensured that all aspects of government were properly taken care of, Musa and Tariq left the region for good in September 714 CE with a huge army, an entourage and thousands of prisoners of war.

Musa was already famous for his speeches and dramatic gestures, and his victorious march to Damascus with thousands of captives had to have been the pinnacle of his glittering military career.

He marched though country after country, often through inhospitable climates, at the head of a triumphant army. In tow, he had many captive European nobles ready to pay homage to the Khalifa at Damascus. Slowly, he made his way overland with hundreds of Visigothic princes, festooned and adorned in their jewels and crowns. This was followed by a procession of slaves, serfs and prisoners of war, all carrying treasures captured in the campaigns.

It must have been an amazing sight as they lumbered through North Africa towards the Middle East. The impressive caravan of people and animals drew gasps of wonder from those who saw them. People waved them by, sometimes stopping one or two to ask what was happening, and sometimes offering food and water as refreshments.

The event brings to mind the marches of the Prophet Sulayman, with his armies of *jinn* and animals, or the victorious marches of Alexander the Great as he travelled through the Himalayas. So awesome was the sight of Musa's convoy as it stretched for mile upon mile that news of it had reached Syria before the procession itself had arrived.

The Arrival in Damascus

Khalifa al-Walid, who was by then very ill and on his death-bed[16], was roused by the news and waited in anticipation to see the incredible spectacle. He ordered a great reception to be held outside the chief mosque at Damascus in honour of his victorious soldiers.

When they finally arrived, in the spring of 715 CE, a sumptuous banquet was held in Musa and Tariq's honour in the courtyard of the great Umayyad Mosque. Courtiers and poets graced the occasion, while Musa related his adventures to the dazzled Khalifa. He was a great orator and showman and so related with relish his campaigns, his strategies, and how he had defeated the enemy.

Then, al-Walid asked to see the results of his campaigns and was shown a long procession of European Royalty, who had been brought forward to pay their respects to the Khalifa. This was the pinnacle of exultant Islam as princes, dukes, nobles and counts came forward to pay homage to the leader of the

---

[16] It is contested among historians whether Musa reached Damascus before or after the death of the Khalifa al-Walid, and some locate the presentation of gifts to the time of the Khalifa Sulayman, al-Walid's brother and heir.

Muslim world. Arab historians have made much of this event from one end of the Islamic lands to the other, and have cited it as one of the glorious moments of the Umayyad period. Indeed it was a curious situation for all concerned. For the first time the Christian lords were able to glimpse how the Muslims dressed and how their courts functioned; likewise, the Muslims were able to see some representatives of Christianity and asked endless questions about the Christian belief of the 'Divinity of Christ'.

The author Ibn Khallikan related the story of how Musa then presented al-Walid with a gift. The gift was a table, fabled to have belonged to the Prophet Sulayman, made for him by the *jinn* who had worked for him. The table, encrusted with semi-precious stones and gold, had remained in Jerusalem for many years until it had been stolen by the Romans, eventually falling into the hands of the Visigoths. Many kings and princes had vied with each other for its possession, as it was rumoured that any man who owned the table would be promised enormous power. Ibn Khallikan writes:

"On this table was gold and silver the like of which one had never seen. Tarik then took off one of its legs together with the gold and pearls it contained and fixed to it a similar leg. The table was valued at 200,000 *dinars* on account of the pearls that were on it. He took up the pearls, the amber, the gold and the silver which he had with him and found a quantity of spoils the like of which one had never seen."

When Tariq had sacked Toledo, he had grasped it from the fleeing Bishop and so brought it back to Damascus as a gift for the Khalifa.

***

PART II

THE LEGACY OF AL-ANDALUS

*"Vale" Tower - **Granada** Alhambra*

CHAPTER SIXTEEN

- The Quest for Knowledge -

With the departure of Musa and Tariq, the Conquest was effectively brought to an end. The two generals had done their part in securing the country and it was now left to those remaining to establish the rule of the Khalifat.

In concluding this portrait of the events that took place when the Iberian Peninsula fell to the Muslims, it would be remiss and highly iniquitous if the beautiful legacy left to Spain in terms of its culture, science, architecture and personalities was not mentioned.

The decaying social and political structure of the Visigothic period had been replaced by a far milder and more equitable system and it became the marvel of the Middle Ages. Although the Hapsburg_Dynasty later destroyed much of this legacy in the sixteenth century, many of the public works still exist today.

We can only imagine what took place in the days of old as one court intrigue followed another in the Alhambra Palace, or as a Berber or Syrian *imam* recited the words of the Glorious Quran in the dusty twilight of a still Granadan night.

"Art, literature and science prospered, as they did nowhere else in Europe. Students flocked from France and Germany[17]

---

[17] Germany as a modern unified country did not exist at this time. A more accurate description would be the 'Germanic lands'; similarly with France.

and England to drink from the fountain of learning, which flowed only in the cities of the Moors. Women were encouraged to devote themselves to serious study and the lady doctor was not unknown among the people of Cordova. Mathematics, astronomy and botany, history philosophy and jurisprudence were to be mastered in Spain and Spain alone... Whatsoever makes a kingdom great and prosperous, whatsoever tends to refinement and civilisation was found in Muslim Spain."[18]

The Legacy Left to Spain

Although the men and women who had devoted their time to such noble pursuits are long gone, it is satisfying to know that at least they have not been forgotten. The richness of some of their works can still be found today in the public libraries, in the museums or in the palatial mansions and gardens that are still scattered widely over Andalusia and other parts of Spain. Poetry had become a key feature of Andalusi culture and was considered to be one of the more refined arts that both scholars and court officials indulged in. Many poems have been translated into different languages and endure today.

The Quest for Knowledge

Education was widely encouraged and one khalifa[19] amassed over 400,000 books for his personal and public libraries. This was at a time when printing had not yet been invented and all books were written by hand.

---

[18] Lane-Poole, Stanley, *The Moors in Spain*, Darf Publishing, London, 1984.

[19] A Khalifat was later established in Andalus for a period of time by 'Abdur Rahman III of Cordoba, a descendant of the Umayyads of Damascus.

*Lion's Courtyard - **Granada** Alhambra*

*Mexuar Court, Detail - **Granada** Alhambra*

Khalifa Hisham had also made his courtiers travel to different parts of the world to find rare manuscripts on a variety of subjects, which included botany, mathematics, poetry and religion. So thorough was he in his scholarly pursuits that sometimes, if he had merely heard of an interesting title, he would ask his men to bring it to him regardless of the distance or cost. If the book could not be moved, he would have it faithfully copied and then have the copy bound and brought back to Andalus. It was through his example, and those of the many others who followed, that education was strongly encouraged in the country.

Cordoba soon became a centre of learning and people would travel to study there from as far afield as England, the Germanic lands, the Balkans or Arabia. As many as seventy public libraries existed, together with extensive street-lighting over the pavements, which encouraged people to read during the evenings. It was one of the few places – one thousand years ago – where literacy had been mastered by the general population, and where unusual subjects could be studied without the normal bigotry and prejudice that had marked the latter part of the Middle Ages.

The Peninsula was the marvel of the Middle Ages and students vied with each other for the honour of sitting at the feet of scholars who pursued varied forms of learning. *Amir* after *amir* patronised the arts, sciences and architecture, whether the reign was prosperous or turbulent.[20]

---

[20] The Prophet Muhammad ﷺ had strongly encouraged learning as a must for all Muslims. It is therefore incumbent upon Muslims to make use of the faculties that Allah has bestowed upon them to seek, learn and to educate others.

CHAPTER SEVENTEEN

- Significant Personalities -

Many famous personalities were born in Andalus. It is difficult to discuss all of them, but there are a few whose influence still affects the modern reader. Among the poets there were Ibn Shuhayd (992-1035 CE), the famous poet and intellectual, and Ibn Hazm (994-1064 CE), an author and vizier who composed the poem *Tawqu-l Hamamah* ('The Ring of the Dove'), which has been translated into many languages. He also wrote the *Kitabu-l Fisal*, a history of religions, which probably had not been equalled by any other writer in the West until the mid-nineteenth century.

Among the mathematicians there was Ibn al-Banna, who did a great deal of work with fractions, as well as Ibn az-Zarqali, who, amongst other things, developed a new astrolabe – the key device used by navigators until the mid-sixteenth century.

Muhammad Ziryab, another personality, though not born in Andalus had migrated there from Baghdad. He taught the ladies of Cordoba about the art of dressing hair under their scarves and created many perfumes, or *'utur*, which were used by the men on their way to the mosques. A celebrated cook and culinary genius, he was also responsible for introducing to Europe the sequential order of eating food, starting with an appetiser and ending with dessert.

The khalifaal historians Ahmad ar-Razi, and his son 'Isa ibn Ahmad ar-Razi, contemporaries of Khalifa 'Abdu-r Rahman III and namesakes of the famous physician, were also natives

Front view of the Mihrab - **Cordoba Mosque**

of Andalus.

In fact, the physician ar-Razi[21] had himself attained celebrity status with the wealthy of Andalus and North Africa, many of whom would travel as far as Baghdad to his chambers for treatment. He had based a great deal of his medicine on the *hadiths*, or traditions of the Prophet ﷺ, and it was he who had been credited for distinguishing smallpox from measles.

However, among the many personalities, there were two particular scholars from Andalus whose fame is worldwide and who were native to this region: Muhyuddin ibn 'Arabi, and Abu'l Walid Muhammad Ibn Rushd.

Ibn 'Arabi (1165-1240 CE)

Ibn 'Arabi was a late tenth century teacher and scholar. He is still read widely today following a resurgence of interest in his writings, and he even has his very own appreciation society based at Oxford University.

He was born in Murcia in southeast Andalus into a family that descended from the famous philanthropist Hatim Tai, and his father had held a position of eminence in the government of Murcia's ruler, Ibn Mardanish.

Ibn 'Arabi's early childhood was spent mainly in academic pursuits, where he excelled under the close supervision of several leading scholars. He often referred to them later in life in the numerous books he was to write. His prodigious mind was apparent from early childhood, and, although merely a

---

[21] Known in European texts as 'Rhazes'.

youth, he would often give intricate and complex discourses on a variety of subjects, including what happens to the soul after death, the *Hadiths*, and the *Shari'ah*.

After the fall of Murcia to the Almohads, his family had moved to Seville and, after a brief stay there, he moved to Cordoba to further pursue his education.

Eventually, Ibn 'Arabi felt the need to travel. This was primarily to perform the pilgrimage to Makkah, and also because a strong desire was burning in him to visit the lands of his ancestors. He resigned from his positions at the many academic institutions he was involved with and left Andalus, never to return.

His first ports of call were the countries of North Africa. Despite his best efforts he was unable to perform the *Hajj* for another few years. En route to Makkah he would often be detained in many of the cities he passed through, as his fame had spread far and wide. Large crowds would assemble to hear his lectures and rarely was he allowed to leave a place before many months had passed. It was during this period that he took to writing and in time he published over five hundred books on a wide range of subjects, though only a handful survive today.

It would not be out of place here to recount an incident that illustrates his nature and the type of man he was. One of his counterparts had been taken ill and Ibn 'Arabi went to see the ailing man to pay his respects. The sick man would not see him and told his wife to tell Ibn 'Arabi that he was intruding in his house and that the best place for him was the local church. On hearing this, Ibn 'Arabi thanked the wife and, after saying a prayer for the sick man, made his way to the church.

The priest on that day was talking of the virtues of Christ, to which Ibn 'Arabi listened with rapt attention until the sermon had reached the stage where the priest referred to Christ as 'the Son of God'. At this point, Ibn 'Arabi stood up and started to speak on the fallacy of this belief. He did so with such eloquence that the priest along with his congregation were mesmerised, as though the truth had been revealed to them for the first time in their lives. He spoke for a while and, when he had finished, everyone stood up – including the priest – and accepted the *Shahadah* at the hands of Ibn 'Arabi.

Thereafter, all the converts marched towards the mosque. As they passed by the house of the sick man, Ibn 'Arabi stopped to thank and bless the man for having sent him to the church, and praised him for saving the souls of so many. Nor was this the first time that misguided souls had found salvation at his hands, for Ibn 'Arabi, by Allah's Good Grace, was instrumental in converting scores of unbelievers.

Although averse to fame, he was unable to contain the increasingly large crowds that gathered around him wherever he went. It has been said that, by the time he reached Makkah, there were thousands of people accompanying him for the Pilgrimage.

It was in Makkah, following the *Hajj*, that he was inspired to write his most famous book, *Futuhatu-l Makkiyyah*, The Makkan Deliberations. A voluminous treatise, it covers religion and faith in a way never before expounded and never quite matched since. The book covers areas such as the nature of the soul, and its origin in relation to its Creator. The question of prophethood is discussed extensively, as is predestination, the Day of Judgement, and, most importantly, elaborate definitions and explanations of the more mystical passages of the Quran. After several years in Arabia he set off again and eventually his travels brought him to Sham (Syria) where he settled to teach. At the zenith of his glory and fame, he passed away on 28th Rabi-u-Thani 638 CE at the age of 78.

Ibn Rushd (1126-1198 CE)

Ibn Rushd, or Averroes as he is known in the West, was also a native of Andalus. He is famous principally for introducing to the West the philosophy underlying the tenets of Islam and for interpreting the works of Aristotle and Plato.

Ibn Rushd was a man of great eminence. He was born in Cordoba in 1126 CE into a renowned family of jurists. His father – at the time a *qadi,* or judge, serving at a court in Cordoba – had trained him in jurisprudence. Shortly after this period he also mastered theology, philosophy and mathematics, all subjects for which he later gained immense prominence throughout the world. He is even acknowledged today as being one of the foremost commentators and interpreters of the philosophies of Aristotle and Plato, which had been taught to him by another scholar, Ibn Tufayl. But not content with this, he also mastered knowledge of medicine under the tutelage of Ibn Zuhr[22].

For the earlier part of his life, he was involved in the Courts of Seville where he rose to the rank of Chief Justice. He later moved to Cordoba to work in the same capacity. Despite his early success as a jurist, his main interest and preoccupation had always been with philosophy – dealing with the nature of the mind and the study of reality and wisdom.

[22] Known in Europe as 'Avenzoar'.

During this period he was introduced to Abu Yaqub Yusuf, the Almohad ruler of Andalus and the Maghrib. Abu Yaqub Yusuf was himself a keen student of philosophy. We are told that during one meeting he asked Ibn Rushd about the creation of the Heavens. There ensued a debate that continued long and hard about the purpose of creation. Ibn Rushd's arguments were so sound that he made a very strong impression on Abu Yaqub Yusuf, and he was thereafter commissioned to translate some of the works of the famous Greek philosophers, most notably Aristotle and Plato. This was the turning point of his career. Despite his demanding duties as Chief Qadi, he completed this task with great success. Subsequently, following the death of his former teacher, he also succeeded Ibn Tufayl as the personal physician to Abu Yaqub Yusuf.

This versatile thinker lived much of his life in controversy, as often happens with people who promote new methods of thinking. His ideas that reason should take precedence over blind faith did not go down well with the advocates of more orthodox methods. However, his spirited arguments on the need for philosophy and logic (the study of the laws of thought and reasoning) to help one gain a deeper and more comprehensive understanding of Islam could not be refuted. Although he was briefly exiled, Abu Yaqub Yusuf's son and successor Ibn Yusuf Yaqub, later reinstated him with full honours.

Apart from his extensive work on the Greek philosophers and his exclusive commentaries on the flaws and logic he saw in their reasoning, he was also famous as a writer on medicine and astronomy. In fact, history recounts the achievements of Ibn Rushd as being in various fields. To the Muslims he is remembered as a great jurist, physician and theologian. To the Christians and Jews he was one of the greatest philosophers of the medieval period – a person who had brought about a complete change to the very meaning of Aristotelian thoughts, which, needless to say, form the bases of modern philosophy. He was also the person who had first promoted to Christian minds the concept of 'dual truths', which led to the eventual segregation of the Christian Church from science. By stating this, he brought about great dissention in Western minds about their faith. Meanwhile to Muslims, Ibn Rushd will live on as an icon who brought refreshing changes and showed ways to view Islam from different angles. He provided a window for those who liked to think.

***

CHAPTER EIGHTEEN

- The Architectural Legacy -

Some of the most beautiful buildings in Spain can still be found in the modern province of Andalusia. Cordoba had rivalled Baghdad as the second most cultured city in the world.

As Victor Robinson, in his book on the story of medicine states:

"Europe was darkened at sunset, Cordova shone with public lamps; Europe was dirty, Cordova built a thousand baths; Europe was covered with vermin, Cordova changed its undergarments daily; Europe lay in mud, Cordova's streets were paved; Europe's palaces had smoke holes in the ceiling, Cordova's arabesques were exquisite; Europe's nobility could not sign its name, Cordova's children went to school; Europe's monks could not read the baptismal service, Cordova's teachers created a library of Alexandrian dimensions[23] ."

In Andalus, the *madhhab* of Malik ibn Anas had largely been adopted and the country functioned according to his orthodox judicial principles. As a result of his beliefs, and those of Islam in general, moderation was encouraged in everyday aspects of life, including the design of buildings and the arts. This can be seen architecturally, where Islamic calligraphy was promoted in the design of buildings as opposed to the use of

---

[23] The Library of Alexandria was famous for its vast collection of works on philosophy, science, and religion, and is reputed to have been the largest and most extensive library in the world until recent history. It was burnt down during the civil wars of the third century, prior to the Muslim conquest in 642 CE.

animals or birds – these had been used quite extensively in the Khalifaal period, but later on, especially under the Almohads, many rulers considered the use of these to be *haram* and instead encouraged simplicity, especially in mosque architecture.

Many of the Muslim rulers of Andalus had spent a great deal of money on public works but without a doubt the ruler to have spent the most money on state buildings was Khalifa 'Abdu-r Rahman III. He spent over one third of the State's revenue to undertake public works. In fact, by the end of the tenth century, according to Arab historians, Cordoba contained over 1,000 mosques, 900 public baths and 80,455 shops. This gives some idea of the size of this great metropolis, thriving at a time when cities like London and Paris were little more than muddy villages.

The Great Mosque of Cordoba

One of the first great rulers of the Peninsula had been 'Abdu-r Rahman I. He ruled from 756-788 CE and took it upon himself to begin building the famous Mosque of Cordoba. This mosque is still standing today, though it was built over 1,200 years ago, and it is truly breathtaking in its splendour. Anyone who is interested in Islamic history and culture should certainly pay it a visit.

'Abdu-r Rahman's rule had seen the construction of a number of important buildings, but certainly the building that has caught the imagination and enthusiasm of countless writers, travellers and admirers is the Great Mosque. Started in 785 CE, it was progressively added to over the next two hundred years.

The main gateway into the mosque was famous for its huge doors. Twenty-one open archways would have allowed worshippers in, while chandeliers holding over a thousand lights further illuminated the way to prayers. 1,293 pillars support numerous arches, which in turn support the roof, all decorated with alternating red and white bricks.[24] The arches, walls, and ceiling would all originally have been painted.

Indeed its fascination for many writers is mainly due to the arrangement of the interior. When entering, many modern visitors are at first confused over which direction to turn in as there are endless vistas in all directions, with no specified walkway in any given direction. One is transfixed by what has best been described over the centuries as "a forest of columns", which grace the imposing interior and spread out in all directions.

A favourite feature of Islamic architecture is the arch and in the Great Mosque there are fifty, each covered in different bands of coloured stone. Inlaid in the stone are complex leaves and floral motifs surrounded by marble, filigree and mosaics, which form the rich decoration.

The *mihrab*, commissioned by the Khalifa al-Hakam II, is resplendently decorated with intricate calligraphy and gold leaf work and it was fashioned by Byzantine craftsmen employed from overseas to do the decoration. Above the *mihrab* is also a dome, which is constructed from a series of entwining sections with a central floral motif, made from the same Byzantine mosaics. Each section holds passages from the

---

[24] The use of different stone made for a much stronger overall structure, providing resistance to earthquakes and the intrusions of later changes. Red and white were also the Umayyad heraldic colours.

Quran, and indeed verses of the Quran frame the *mihrab* itself vividly painted in gold and blue. Some of the phrases are still easily legible today.[25]

The Mosque is also famous for its *minbar,* which once stood on the left-hand side of the mosque but sadly no longer survives. This was where the *imam* would have given his *khutbah,* or sermon. The *minbar* itself was made from seasoned wood, including sandalwood and cedar, and was constructed from 36,000 different pieces of varying colours, shapes and textures. These were then painstakingly pieced together to give an overall dazzling effect. Cordoban craftsmen had built another famous *minbar* for the Kutubiyyah Mosque in Marrakech and it is now housed in the El Badi Palace Museum there. This is perhaps the only surviving example of an Andalusi *minbar* and, though much smaller, it might well provide us with an idea of how the original Cordoba Minbar would have looked.

Four enormous fountains, equipped with water brought down from the mountains by a system of underground irrigation, supplied worshippers with clean water with which to do their ablutions. The twinkling of running water could be heard throughout the day and night and was a faithful reminder to the congregation that prayer-time was not far off.[26]

In Islam, a mosque is not just a place of worship, but has many other functions. It is a place for meetings and gatherings,

[25] Some of the Kufic mosaics that frame the *mihrab* were destroyed when an altar - placed there later by the Christians then using the building as a church - was pulled out, bringing away sections of the mosaics with it.

[26] One chronicler also said that the sound of Andalus was "the sound of running water".

education, respite and the exchange of information. The Great Mosque served all these functions. On one side, towards the Khalifa's Palace, there were quarters built to offer travellers rest and shelter. The Mosque also served food to wandering travellers, hospitality being a fundamental duty according to the tenets of Islam.

Today, the outside of the Mosque is strangely deceptive as it appears rather plain and disguises the fact that inside there is an awesome building with pillars that seem to go on forever. It is easy, as one walks through the broody silent interior, to become lost in the cool dignity of the place and wonder about the many celebrated personalities who must have walked past these very columns, lost in their religious thoughts.

Sadly, the Great Mosque was turned into a cathedral in the sixteenth century. The Cathedral occupies the entire central area of the Mosque, looking out of place in the midst of the columns and among the rest of the decoration. When Charles V was brought to admire it, his famous comment was, "If I had known what you wished to do, you would not have done it, because what you are carrying out there is to be found elsewhere, and what you had formerly does not exist anywhere else in the world."[27]

The Alhambra

Undoubtedly one of the most frequently visited tourist sites in Andalusia today is the Alhambra Palace, whose name comes from the Arabic *Al Qal'atu-l Hamra*, meaning 'The Red Castle'.

---

[27] Charles V, the Catholic monarch then ruling what became 'Spain', had originally given his permission for the Cathedral to be built.

Situated on one of Granada's hills, and lying just 50 miles inland from the Mediterranean, its site cast a spell over the Muslims. The name 'Alhambra' was coined because of the iron-rich soil that was used to construct it, which is red in colour.[28] Cool, fragrant and aloof it stands some 3,000 feet above sea level like a sentinel, on the hilltops beneath the distant presence of the Sierra Nevada Mountains.

Frequently referred to as 'the Acropolis of Granada', one of the unique features of the Alhambra is that no expensive metals were used in its construction or beautification. Built in the fourteenth century over the site of a previous 'Alcazaba' by Yusuf I of the Nasrid Dynasty, and later by Muhammad V, its survival is due largely to chance and good fortune rather than to a calculated effort to preserve something unique to Southern Spain. In fact, it is one of the few remaining examples of Medieval Islamic architecture that are left in Europe. Nevertheless its design, layout, sparkling fountains and landscaped gardens have enchanted many European visitors, including King Ferdinand and Queen Isabella of Spain, who made it their private retreat during visits to Granada.

Its charm is due to a common theme in Islamic buildings, where an unassuming exterior contrasts with a richly decorated interior. This provided its residents with the satisfaction of having a private retreat, with a brilliantly but unexpected dazzling centre. In the Alhambra there is a fusion of different architectural styles, which have been blended together to produce one cohesive whole. In addition, Muslim architecture favours patios, landscaped gardens, portico

---

[28] It is said that the Alhambra also took its name from the Nasrid ruler who had restored it; he himself was known as 'Yusuf Al-Ahmar', or 'Yusuf the Red'.

entrances, and an extensive use of water – as well as large airy rooms with bright, complex designs that are rich in ornamentation. These were all used to perfection in the Alhambra. Here, the interior and exterior seem to glide and merge into each other, so that they appear to be connected in one smooth uninterrupted fashion.

The Palace can be approached by a series of winding roads, which lead up to the front entrance. It has a number of impressive sections, including the Court of Myrtles, the Court of Lions and the elaborately decorated Hall of the Two Sisters.

The Court of Myrtles is so called because of the myrtle trees that used to surround it. The Court itself is 140 feet long and 70 feet wide. In its centre lies a large pond where water lilies vie for space, and which is framed by rows of miniature twisted cypresses. A calm and graceful enclosure, it was used in the days of old by laureates to compose their thoughtful treatises in praise of Allah, and poems border the walls all around the courtyard.

To three of its sides are rooms with exquisite arabesques, some of which hold with weighty decorated ceilings in stucco relief. All walls repeat the same motto in sophisticated designs, 'There is no conqueror but Allah'. Other ceilings are bordered with poems celebrating the magnificence of the seven heavens and all that lies between them.

Further along is the striking Court of the Lions, which was re-introduced to the world in more recent times by the writings of Washington Irving after his famous sojourn there in 1829. Here, 128 marble columns, grouped in threes and fours, support an enclosed space, which is somewhat smaller than the Court of Myrtles. Each stylised wall is inscribed with delicate stucco relief while above them runs a fresco, made of cedarwood that travels around the entire courtyard. In the centre lies the enchanting little fountain, where twelve marble lions still spout their water, as if uninterrupted for centuries.[29]

A Hapsburg King who came to view the Alhambra after it was captured from the Muslims, poignantly stated, "Ill-fated was the man who lost all this!"

***

[29] Not all of the lions are original, some now sit in a museum in Madrid.

CHAPTER NINETEEN

- Almeria's Silk Industry -

The whole of Southern Spain is dotted with small towns, fortresses and ruins, which are a reminder of their former glory. One such place is Almeria, which lies in the district of the same name, and which was originally famous for its great Umayyad fortress, the Alcazaba, but of which little survives today.

Close to the coast, nestling near the foot of the Alpujarras Mountains, it lies about 150 miles to the east of Malaga. A one-time small provincial town, it was brought to life by the combined industry of the local people and the Muslims, who had seen its potential as a centre for the production and manufacture of silk.

Silk itself is an ancient fabric, having been used for thousands of years as a luxurious and durable natural fibre, which can be woven into many different styles and dyed into an amazing array of colours. The Muslims had brought many of their skills with them when they arrived in the Iberian Peninsula, and they quickly realised that the manufacture of silk would be a profitable and lucrative industry. The Europeans craved the luxury of possessing oriental fabrics and the silk could easily be exported all over Europe because the climate, soil and terrain of the areas surrounding the Alpujarras Mountains were ideal for the raising of silk worms and the mulberry bushes from which they feed.

Due to the light weight of the cocoons, vast quantities would be shipped to different places for manufacture. They were transported on the backs of donkeys, which could easily travel through the rough terrain of the mountains. The silk was then woven into various fabrics including damask, georgian and camlet. Dyes from plant extracts were used, and the fabrics were exported to every part of the known world. It was a hugely profitable industry and was responsible for turning Almeria into the second richest city in Europe.

Unfortunately, as happened with so many of the industries of Andalus, once the Muslims had been expelled from the region, the silk industry collapsed, and – as with Valencia – the economy suffered along with it, leading to widespread starvation in the hinterland. Sadly, Almeria today is simply a regional city dependent upon tourism as one of its mainstays. Such was the tragic conclusion to a once prosperous and thriving region.

**

EPILOGUE

Here ends the story of the capture and transformation of Visigothic Iberia into Al-Andalus. This narrative only provides a synopsis of the actual Conquest and, to a lesser extent, the legacy left to Spanish culture.

After the Conquest, followed a glorious period when Andalus flourished for many hundreds of years under her Muslim leaders. However, that story must be left for another occasion, when the years spent in the material development of the region can be discussed more comprehensively, along with the overall effects that these had on the country until eventually the Muslims had been driven out.

All civilisations have their moments of glory, victory and success, and then demise and destruction set in. It, too, happened in Andalus in the lead up to 1492 CE. However, in throwing the Muslims out, the new Spaniards had, in the words of one writer, realised too late "that they had killed the goose that laid their golden egg". Many profitable industries collapsed, the economy suffered, libraries were burnt, mosques closed and public baths destroyed, as they were too reminiscent of the rank infidel.

One church leader, Cardinal Ximenes, ordered the burning of thousands of the manuscripts that had been so meticulously pieced together over many years. These manuscripts had represented the best in Islamic research and learning and had taken years to compile.

All this was done in order to destroy the heritage left by the 'heathen', but the plan was not quite effective. Writer after writer, whether Muslim or Christian, has sung the praises of Andalus, while at the same time mourned the annihilation of a civilisation that had brought prosperity and peace to a poor agricultural region of Europe.

In the words of the Orientalist Stanley Lane-Poole:

"The misguided Spaniards knew not what they were doing... For centuries Spain had been the centre of civilisation, the seat of arts and sciences, of learning and every form of refined enlightenment. No other country in Europe had so far approached the cultivated dominion of the Moors. The true memorial of the Moors is seen in desolate tracts of utter barrenness, where once the Muslims grew luxuriant vines and olives and yellow ears of corn; is [seen in] a stupid ignorant population where once wit and learning flourished; is [seen in] the general stagnation and degradation of a people which has hopelessly fallen in the scale of the nations and has deserved its humiliation."

In order that the Muslims too do not forget their incredible past it is incumbent upon all of them to remember, and pass on to future generations the knowledge that has been gained through this story – so that, if nothing else, the oft-repeated accusation that Muslims are barbarian conquerors can finally be counteracted with the truth.

***

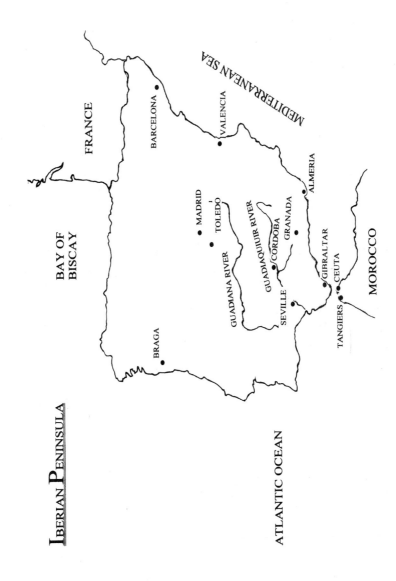

IBERIAN PENINSULA

FRANCE

BAY OF
BISCAY

BARCELONA

VALENCIA

MEDITERRANEAN SEA

ALMERIA

MADRID

TOLEDO

GUADIAQUIUR RIVER

GRANADA

CORDOBA

GIBRALTAR

GUADIANA RIVER

SEVILLE

CEUTA

TANGIERS

MOROCCO

BRAGA

ATLANTIC OCEAN

115

GLOSSARY
of principal terms, names and places

[This glossary does not include the more obvious terms used, nor the very obscure, and it does not include those already explained in the main text.]

A

A.H. – 'Anno Hegirae' or 'In the Year of the Hijrah'. The Muslim calendar starts with the emigration or Hijrah from Makkah to Madinah in 622 CE.

Abu Bakr as-Siddiq (c.571/2 - 634 CE) – Cousin and close Companion of the Prophet Muhammad ﷺ. The first Khalifa following his death.

Acropolis – An Ancient Greek temple complex in Athens.

Alcazaba (*al-qasabah*) – 'Fortified castle' or 'citadel'.

Alexander the Great – Macedonian ruler; conquered much of south-eastern Europe, Asia Minor, the Near East, Mesopotamia, and parts of India.

Algeciras (*Al-Jaziratu-l Khudra'*) – Meaning 'the Green Peninsula', Algeciras is one of Spain's southern coastal cities.

Almeria (*Al-Maryah*) – Meaning 'the Mirror [of the Sea]'.

Almohad (*Al-Muwahidun*) – A Berber dynasty that invaded in 1147 CE and ruled most of Morocco and much of Al-Andalus. They re-established Muslim control over the Peninsula.

Almoravid (*Al-Murabitun*) – A Berber dynasty that invaded in 1086 CE. They drove out initial encroachments made by Christian forces.

Las Alpujarras – A circuit of mountainous hills and valleys just south of Granada and the Sierra Nevada Mountain range.

amir – 'Ruler' or 'Commander'.

Amiru-l Mu'mineen – 'Commander of the Faithful'. This is an honorific title given to the Khalifa.

Al-Andalus, **or Andalus** – The name given to the whole of the Iberian Peninsula that came under Muslim rule, including modern Portugal, modern Spain and parts of Southern France.

Andalusia – A semi-autonomous region of modern Spain. 'Andalusia' as a term by no means equates to 'Andalus' or 'Muslim Spain'.

Aragon – Province in the north of Spain; later under the control of King Ferdinand, who captured Granada in 1492 CE.

Arian (Christianity) – A pre-Catholic variant of Christianity common in Europe at this time; Unitarian in its beliefs, it rejected the Trinity.

Assyria – An ancient kingdom in the Mesopotamian region.

Astoria or 'the Asturias' – A region near Leon and Aragon in the North. It was from Covadonga that Pelayo caused disruption.

Augustus Caesar – The First Roman Emperor, who ruled much of the Europe, and also parts of Asia Minor, North Africa and the Middle East.

'Abdu-l 'Aziz ibn Musa – Son of Musa ibn Nusayr, and first Governor of Al-Andalus. He campaigned in Portugal; took Pamplona, Malaga and Granada. He was assassinated in 716 CE.

'Abdu-r Rahman I ('ad-Dakhil') – Grandson and heir of the last Umayyad Khalifa in Damascus, he escaped the Abbasid slaughter of his family; fled to Al-Andalus, where he was proclaimed Amir in 756 CE.

'Abdu-r Rahman III ('an-Nasir li-Deeni-l Llah') – The eighth Umayyad ruler of Al-Andalus, he established the Andalusi Khalifat in Cordoba in 929 CE.

'Abdu-r Rahman ibn 'Abdullah al-Ghafiqi – He became the fifth and eleventh governor of Al-Andalus after the initial conquests.

'Ali ibn Abi Talib (c.598 - 661 CE) – Cousin and son-in-law of the Prophet ﷺ. The fourth Khalifa, he was assassinated by a Kharijite faction.

'Amr ibn al-'As (d. 665 CE) – A general in Syria under Abu Bakr; Governor of Palestine for 'Umar, and the conqueror of Egypt.

'Anbasah ibn Suhaym – The sixth governor of Al-Andalus following Abdu-r Rahman al-Ghafiqi.

B

Babylon – An ancient kingdom of the Mesopotamian region.

Baghdad – The capital of the Abbasid Khalifat.

Basques – A people of unknown origin (related to Celts, Berbers and Chechens) that inhabits the north-eastern part of the Peninsula. Many of the Umayyad Amirs and Khalifas were married to Basque women.

Bay of Biscay – A turbulent stretch of the Atlantic Ocean off the coast of France and Spain.

Berbers – The indigenous peoples of the North African region who had their own empire in pre-Islamic times. Of unknown origin, they are linked to the Basques and to the Celts of Western Britain.

Bilal ibn Rabah (d. 642 CE) – An Abyssinian client of Abu Bakr as-Siddiq. He was the first to give the adhan. He was at the side of the Prophetﷺ at all of his battles, and at the side of Abu Bakr when he died.

Bourbon (Dynasty) – A later Christian dynasty that ruled Spain in the eighteenth century.

Byzantine (Empire) – The Christian successor empire of the Romans, whose capital was in Constantinople (modern day Istanbul).

C

C.E. – 'Common Era'. The politically correct term referring to the Christian dating system, which begins after the official birth of Jesus.

Ceuta (*Sebta*) – A port off the coast of Morocco, facing the southern coast of Spain.

Charles V (Emperor) – Charles became Emperor of the Holy Roman Empire in 1521CE; ruled Spain and much of the rest of Europe.

Columbus, Christopher – The explorer who 'discovered' the Americas in 1492 CE, helped by a Muslim navigator and pre-drawn maps in Arabic.

Companions – The Companions of the Prophetﷺ.

Constantine (Emperor) – The first Roman Emperor to convert to Christianity, but on his deathbed; he became an Arian not a Catholic.

Cordoba (*Qurtubah*) – An important city lying northeast of Seville and on the Guadalquivir river. The illustrious Muslim capital of the Umayyads, it was conquered by the Christians in 1236 CE, and then sank into decline.

Curiales – From the Latin *curiae*.

D

Damascus – The oldest known city in the world, and the capital of Syria. Home to the Umayyad Dynasty.

dinar – A gold coin of the Islamic currency system at this time.

dirham – A silver coin of the Islamic currency system at this time.

Diwan – The administration ledgers, or 'accounts', of the government; came to mean the administrative body of the government.

E

El-Badi (Palace) – An old palace fortress found in Marrakesh, built in 1578 CE. Now mostly ruined, it is said to have once inspired poets.

Elvira – An historical Muslim city that no longer exists, but that was once an important neighbouring industrial city to Granada.

F

Ferdinand (King of Aragon) – The fifth king of Aragon, one of the powerful Christian regions in the Iberian Peninsula during the fifteenth century. He married Isabella of Castille.

Florinda – The daughter of Julian of Ceuta. Chroniclers also show she was called 'Cava' from the Arabic '*qahbah*', meaning whore. Perhaps Roderick's supporters had been trying to pin the blame on her.

G

Gengis Khan (c.1167–1227 CE) – The Mongol leader who unified the peoples of the Steppe, and led his hordes across the Middle and Near East. The Mongol Empire eventually stretched from Hungary to Korea. Many of his decendents became Muslims.

Gibraltar (*Jabalu-t Tariq*) – Meaning 'Tariq's Mountain'. The point of Tariq ibn Ziyad's initial landing. The stretch of sea between Tangiers and Gibraltar is thus known as 'the Straits of Gibraltar'.

Granada (*Gharnatah*) – An important city for the Umayyads, Almohads and the Almoravids, it came to prominence when the Nasrids fled south in the 1240s. The last Muslim stronghold, housing hundreds of thousands of refugees from all over the Peninsula.

Guadalquivir (*Al-Wadi Al-Kabir*) – Meaning 'the Great [River] Valley'. It was from this river that Muslims sourced their irrigation schemes and it was a navigable waterway in earlier times.

H

Hajib – 'Chamberlain'. He ruled on behalf of the Khalifa as a sort of Prime Minister or Chancellor.

Al-Hakam II (Khalifa) – The second Umayyad Khalifa of Al-Andalus, who built extensions to the Great Mosque of Cordoba, and also completed the city of Madina Azahara.

Hapsburg (Dynasty) – The successor dynasty to the family of Isabella and Ferdinand; ruled Spain, other parts of Europe, and the American colonies, in the sixteenth century; Charles V was a Hapsburg.

Hatim Tai – King of the Banu Tai who occupied the Najd and who later converted to Islam. An ancestor of the scholar Muhyiddin Ibn 'Arabi.

Heristal, Pepin – He ruled all the Frankish kingdoms except Aquitaine.

Hisham II (Khalifa) (962-1016 CE) – The tenth Umayyad Khalifa of Al-Andalus, and son of Al-Hakam II.

Hispania – This is the Latin term for the parts of the Iberian Peninsula that came under the Roman Empire. The modern word 'Spain' is derived from this term.

I

Ibn al-Banna – Abu'l-Abbas Ahmad ibn Muhammad ibn 'Uthman al-Azdi. It is not known whether he was born in Marrakesh or Granada, but spent most of his life in Merenid Morocco; specialised in geometry, fractions, algebra and astronomy; dates are not known for sure.

Ibn al-Quttiyah (d. 978 CE) – Meaning 'Son of the Gothic Lady'; historian of the Muslim Conquest; a descendant of Countess Sara, who had supported Umayyad 'Abdu-r Rahman I.

Ibn az-Zarqali, Abu Ishaq Ibrahim ibn Yahya (1028-1087 CE) – Known as 'Arzachel'; a great astrologer of Cordoba; proved the movement of the solar apogee; developed the 'Toledan Tables', a mapping of the planetary tables; wrote a treatise on trigonometrical tables.

Ibn Hazm, Abu Muhammad 'Ali ibn Ahmad ibn Sa'id (994-1064 CE) – A Cordoban theologian, and soldier of the Umayyad cause. Originally a Shafi'i jurist, he adopted Zahiri thinking; wrote extensively on the Muslim character, on *fiqh*, grammar, and the principles of jurisprudence; and he wrote the famous love-poem, *Tawqu-l Hamamah*.

Ibn Khallikan, Ahmad ibn Muhammad (1211-1282 CE) – An 'Iraqi judge and famous biographer of Muslim heroes and personalities. His huge encyclopaedia has a whole section on Al-Andalus.

Ibn Mardanish, Muhammad ibn Sa'd (1146-1172 CE) – An Almoravid ruler, originally of Murcia, and who also became the ruler of Valencia. He was ousted by the Almohads.

Ibn Shuhayd, Abu 'Amir Ahmad ibn 'Abdu-l Malik (992/3-1035 CE) – An Andalusi physician, and also an important prose writer of his time.

Ibn Tufayl, Abu Bakr Muhammad (1110-1185 CE) – Known as 'Abubacer'. Born in Guadix (*Wadi 'Ash*) near Granada. He was an important philosopher, and a poet. Most notably, he was a Court physician. His famous philosophical romance was *Hayy ibn Yaqzan*.

Ibn Zuhr, Abu Marwan 'Abdu-l Malik (1091-1161 CE) – Known as 'Avenzoar'. From Seville; a brilliant physician and clinician; developed a number of medical theories; the first parasitologist; experimented with techniques such as tracheotomy; wrote on diet and also psychology.

Ifriqiya - This had been the Roman Province of 'Africa' and mainly it referred to what is modern day Tunisia.

Isabella (Queen of Castille) – Ruler of a powerful Christian region in the fifteenth century; responsible for the capture of Granada in 1492 CE and ruler of Christian Spain thereafter.

J

Julian – He has also been called 'Ilyan', 'Urban' and 'Olban'. It is said that he was a Berber Christian.

K

kafir (pl. *kuffar*) – One who rejects belief.

Khalid ibn al-Walid – One of the warriors of the Quraysh. He was sent to 'Iraq by Abu Bakr and was one of his generals in Syria.

Khalifa (*khalifah*) – Meaning 'successor' or 'representative', referring to the successors of Muhammad ﷺ. The Muslim ruler that has jurisdiction over the entire Muslim world.

Khalifat (*Khilafah*) – The office or jurisdiction of the Khalifa.

khutbah – speech or sermon.

Kutubiyyah – An Almohad mosque in Marrakech, the style of which is very similar to the original mosques of Al-Andalus.

L

Lakhm, Lakhmid – A pre-Islamic tribal confederation that guarded the Arabian frontiers as a client-state to the Sasanian Empire.

Latifundia – The Roman Upper Classes, which were dominated by the military elites.

Levant – The central Middle Eastern region stretching from Palestine through to the west of 'Iraq.

M

madhhab (pl. *madhahib*) – Literally 'a way that is travelled' or 'a system that is followed'. Refers to the four Sunni schools of jurisprudence (*fiqh*), which provide Muslims with easily-accessible guidebooks on how they should live their lives in accordance with Islam.

Al-Maghrib, the Maghrib – The North African region. It is also the modern Arabic word for Morocco specifically.

Makkah – The birthplace of the Prophet Muhammadﷺ and Islam's most holy city; where Muslims go for their pilgrimage (*Hajj*); located in the area now occupied by Saudi Arabia.

Malaga (*Malaqah*) – Coastal city and port on the southern tip of Spain.

Malik ibn Anas, Abu 'Abdullah (712-795 CE) – From Madinah; became the principle influence in the formulation of early Islamic Law; the principal founder of the Maliki *madhhab*, and transmitter of *hadiths*.

Marrakesh – A city in the south of Morocco bordering the High Atlas. Founded in the late eleventh century, it was an Almohad stronghold.

Martel, Charles – 'Charles the Hammer', after whom the Carolingian dynasty is named. In 719 CE, he became King of the Franks. Grandfather of Charlemagne, a later bete noire for the Muslim world.

Mesopotamia – A Greek word, meaning '[a region] between the two rivers', that is the Euphrates and the Tigris; refers to the region now occupied by 'Iraq, Kuwait and parts of Turkey.

mihrab – The prayer niche at the front of the mosque where the *imam* stands to lead the prayer, facing Makkah.

minbar – The pulpit upon which the *imam* stands to give his sermons.

'Moors' – A corruption of the Latin *mauri*, referring to inhabitants of the Roman province of Mauretania. Used inaccurately to refer to all of the Muslim peoples who came to the Iberian Peninsula.

Mu'awiya ibn Abi Sufyan (- 680 CE) – Companion; the Prophet's ﷺ scribe; became Umayyad Khalifa in Damascus; Khalifa number five (not counting Hassan ibn 'Ali); fought 'Ali at Siffin over a political matter, but they later made amends.

Mughith – Greek client of the Khalifa al-Walid; he captured Cordoba.

Murcia – A silk-farming region; the main date-growing region.

N

Napoleon – Self-proclaimed emperor of France at the end of the eighteenth century, and early nineteenth; expanded French dominions as far as Egypt and India.

Nasrid (Dynasty) – A Muslim kingship originating from Zaragoza; they fled south and re-established in Granada; responsible for two of Islam's great architectural heritage sites, the Aljaferia and the Alhambra.

Nebuchadnezzar (c. 630-561 BC) – Nebuchadnezzar II, King of Babylon; conquered Syria and Israel; fought the Egyptians; subdued the Phoenicians. The Babylonian kingdom became a powerful force in the Mesopotamian region.

P

Pelayo – Rebel leader, perhaps legendary, active in the Asturias who organised resistance movements against Muslim rulers.

Persia, Persian (Empire) – Also known as the Sasanian Empire; pre-Islamic rival to the Romans; defeated by Khalid ibn al-Walid at the Battle of Qadisiyyah; Empire had covered parts of Central Asia, Iran, 'Iraq, Syria, the Yemen and eastern provinces of Saudi Arabia.

Phoenicians – A sea-born trading 'empire' that pre-dated the Romans, but also contemporary; established out-posts in the Mediterranean and the Near and Middle East, such as at Carthage in modern Tunisia.

Poitiers (Battle of) – Also known as 'the Battle of Tours'; the Franks halted the Muslim advance further into 'France' in 732 CE; al-Ghafiqi killed. Poitiers is just south of Paris.

Portugal – The western most region of the Iberian Peninsula, formerly known as *Al-Gharb*. Possibly from where the modern Arabic word for orange, '*burtuqal*', originates.

The Pyrenees – One of the highest and most impregnable mountain ranges in the world; bordering southern France and northern Spain.

Q

qadi – judge or jurisprudential expert

R

Rajab – Seventh month in the Muslim calendar; it was during this month that the Prophet Muhammad ﷺ made his night journey into Paradise.
Ar-Razi ('Rhazes'), Abu Bakr Muhammad ibn Zakariya (841-926 CE) – Born in Persia; one of the greatest physicians of history; a main influence on Western medical theory; an alchemist; 'the father of Pediatrics'; established and ran the teaching hospital in Baghdad.

Reccared (King) – Visigothic king of the 580s who became Catholic and whose conversion saw the end to Arian Christianity in the region.

Roman (Empire) – Dominated Europe, much of the Near and Middle East for four centuries in varying forms; previously a 'Republic' dating from circa 200 BC; collapsed as an effective force with the invasion of the Huns in 410 CE; transmogrified into the Catholic 'Holy Roman Empire'.

S

Sahabah – 'Companions [of the Prophet Muhammad ﷺ]', that is those who were alive during his lifetime.

'Saracen' – A Frankish term derived from '*al-Sharqiyyeen*', 'the Easterners'; used by the Crusaders to refer to the Arabs of the Levant.

Seville (*Ishbiliyyah*) – One of the first Muslim capitals; also the Almoravid capital much later; is said to have had the largest mosque in Al-Andalus; the famous Giralda is what is left of the Almohad minaret and observatory; the city fell in 1248 CE to Christian forces.

Sham – Essentially the area surrounding Damascus; some take it to mean the wider Syrian territories stretching to the Mediterranean, and taking in Al-Quds (Jerusalem).

Sierra Morena – A long mountain range in the south of Spain. It cuts off the northern border of Cordoba from the province of Castille.

Sierra Nevada – A mountain range outside Granada.

Spain – This is a modern Iberian country. 'Spain' is only used in this book to refer to the modern borders (unless as part of a quotation from a clumsy historian).

Stalin – Meaning 'Steel'; the *nom-de-guerre* of Communist dictator of the Soviet Union and sociopath Josef Vissiaronovich Djugashvili.

Sulayman (Prophet) – The Prophet Solomon in Judeo-Christian theology; he had command over the winds, could understand the language of animals and plants; his army consisted of both men and *jinn*.

T

Tangiers (*Tanja*) – A city and port on the north coast of Morocco.

Tarifa (*Jaziratu-t Tarif*) – Meaning 'Tarif's Headland'. Now a modern town; the site of the first landing under the leadership of Tarif ibn Malik.

Tarif ibn Malik – A Berber freedman of Musa ibn Nusayr.

Tariq ibn Ziyad – A freedman of Musa ibn Nusayr; *Akhbar Majmu'ah* has him as a Persian from Hamadan, others say he was a Berber.

Toledo (*Tulaytulah*) – Visigothic capital; accustomed to rebellion; brought into line by 'Abdu-r Rahman III; city of sciences and intellect; important historically for the Jews.

Trinity (Doctrine of) – Now a fundamental Christian belief that God as 'The Father' is in divine union with Jesus Christ as 'The Son', with the 'Holy Spirit' as the third entity. Since the Council of Nicaea in 325 CE, it has been progressively enforced on the Christian world.

U

Ummah – Meaning 'people' or 'nation'; from the same route for 'mother' and '*imam*'; the term used to describe the global Muslim community, and its joint responsibilities.

Umayyad (Dynasty) – The family of the Bani Umayyah – a branch of the Quraysh – who established the *khilafah* in Damascus and ruled the Muslim world for some generations. Both third khalifa 'Uthman, and fifth khalifa Mu'awiya were from this family.

'Umar ibn al-Khattab (c.583 - 644 CE) – The second Khalifa; appointed successor of Abu Bakr; Qurayshi; assassinated in 23 AH.

'Uthman ibn 'Affan (c.576 – 656 CE) – The elected third Khalifa; twice son-in-law of Muhammad ﷺ; Umayyad; assassinated in 35 AH.

'utur (**sing.** *'itr*) – Perfumes.

W

Wadi Bekka – Valley of unknown location; perhaps the Rio Salado.

wala' – Meaning 'clientage'; a 'client' or 'freed slave', was a *mawla*.

Al-Walid ibn 'Abdu-l Malik (Khalifa) – Sixth Umayyad Khalifa; ruled from 705-715 CE; reconstructed Great Mosque of Madinah; built Al-Aqsa and the Dome of the Rock in Jerusalem, and the Great Mosque in Damascus; established Umayyad alliance with Witiza's family.

Witiza (King) – Also known as 'Witica' by other chroniclers.

X

Ximenes (Cardinal) – Ruthless practitioner of the Spanish Inquisition; original name, Ben Shimon; himself the victim of a forced conversion from Judaism to Catholicism.

Z

Zannata – A Berber tribe who had welcomed the fugitive 'Abdu-r Rahman when he fled the Abbasids.

Ziryab, Muhammad – Persian musician; added the fifth string to the lyre (*'oud*); introduced the use of crystal tableware; a favourite confidant of Amir 'Abdu-r Rahman II (822-852 CE).

BIBLIOGRAPHY

1. The Holy Qur'an
2. Ali, Syed Amir, *A Short History of the Arabs*,
   Kitab Bhavan, New Delhi, 1994
3. Creasy, Edward, *Fifteen Decisive Battles of the World*,
   E.P. Dutton & Co, New York
4. Dozy, Rheinhart, *Muslims in Spain*,
   Darf Publishing, London, 1988
5. Gill, A. A. & Curtis, Benjamin, *The Best of Spain*,
   Travel Intelligence Ltd., 2002
6. Grans, David J., *Portugal*, Cadogan Guides, 1990
7. Harvey, Maurice, *Gibraltar*, Spellmaint Ltd., 1996
8. Hitti, Philip K., *History of the Arabs*,
   Macmillan, London, 1994
9. Home, Charles F., *The Sacred Books and Early Literature of the East*, Parke Austin & Lipscomb, New York, 1917
10. Ibn Abdel Hakem, translated by John Harris Jones, *History of the Conquest of Spain*, Gottingen W. F. Kaestner, 1858
11. Irving, Thomas Ballantine (Al-Hajj Ta'leem 'Ali Abu Nasr), *Falcon of Spain: A Study of Eight Century Spain, With Special Emphasis Upon the Life of the Umayyad Ruler 'Abdurrahman I (756-788)*, Sh. Muhammad Ashraf Publishers, Lahore, 1991
12. Lane-Poole, Stanley, *The Moors in Spain*,
    Darf Publishing, London, 1984
13. Various writers, *The World of Islam*,
    Thames and Hudson, London, 1994
14. Vryoris, Speros, *Byzantium and Europe*,
    Thames & Hudson, London, 1967

***